2·08

LUXURY
HOME PLANS

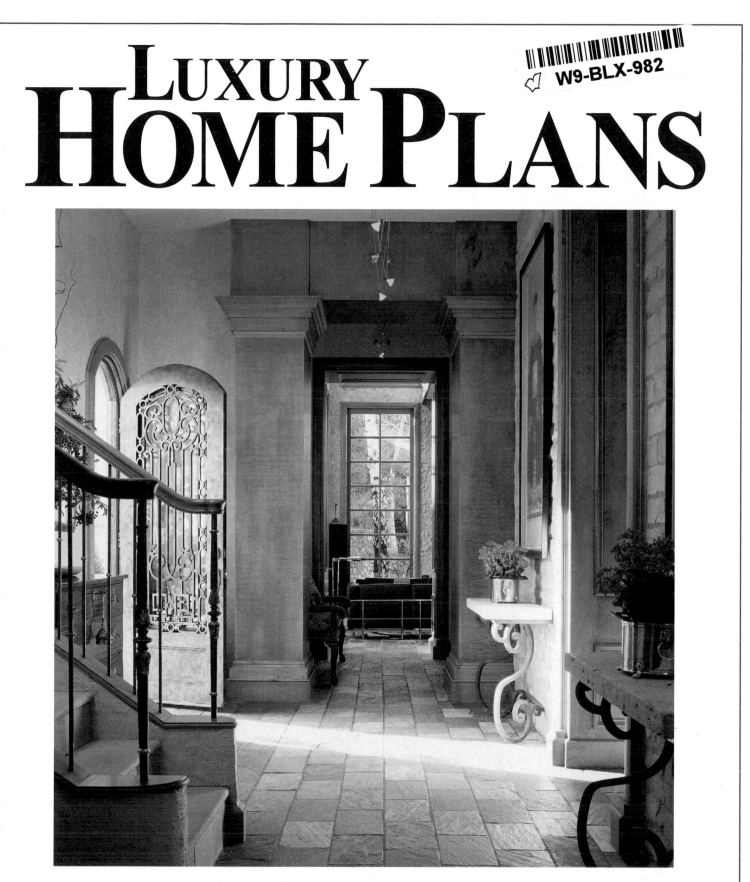

150 *Finely Crafted* Home Designs

Luxury HOME PLANS

12

Published by Hanley Wood
One Thomas Circle, NW, Suite 600
Washington, DC 20005

Distribution Center
PBD
Hanley Wood Consumer Group
3280 Summit Ridge Parkway
Duluth, Georgia 30096

Vice President, Home Plans, Andrew Schultz
Associate Publisher, Editorial Development, Jennifer Pearce
Managing Editor, Hannah McCann
Editor, Simon Hyoun
Assistant Editor, Kimberly Johnson
Publications Manager, Brian Haefs
Production Manager, Melissa Curry
Director, Plans Marketing, Mark Wilkin
Senior Plan Merchandiser, Nicole Phipps
Plan Merchandiser, Hillary Huff
Graphic Artist, Joong Min
Plan Data Team Leader, Susan Jasmin
Marketing Director, Holly Miller
Marketing Manager, Bridgit Kearns

Most Hanley Wood titles are available at quantity discounts with bulk purchases for educational, business, or sales promotional use. For information, please contact Andrew Schultz at aschultz@hanleywood.com.

BIG DESIGNS, INC.
President, Creative Director, Anthony D'Elia
Vice President, Business Manager, Megan D'Elia
Vice President, Design Director, Chris Bonavita
Editorial Director, John Roach
Senior Art Director, Stephen Reinfurt
Production Director, David Barbella
Photo Editor, Christine DiVuolo
Graphic Designer, Frank Augugliaro
Graphic Designer, Billy Doremus
Production Manager, Rich Fuentes

PHOTO CREDITS
Front Cover: See Design HPK2400001. Photo by Sam Gray. Back Cover (Clockwise from top): HPK2400041 on page 56, photo by Russell Kingman; HPK2400026 on page 41, photo by Kim Sargent; HPK2400054 on page 69, photo by Exposures Unlimited, Ron and Donna Kolb; HPK2400040 on page 55, photo by Joseph Lapeyra; HPK2400001 on page 12, photo by Ahmann Design, Inc.

10 9 8 7 6 5 4 3 2 1

Printed in the United States of America

Library of Congress Control Number: 2006925825

ISBN-13: 978-1-931131-63-6
ISBN-10: 1-931131-63-5

126

72

Contents

ONLINE EXTRA!

Hanley Wood Passageway

The Hanley Wood Passageway is an online search tool for your home plan needs! Discover even more useful information about building your new home, search additional new home plans, access online ordering, and more at www.hanleywoodbooks.com/ luxuryhomeplans

hanley▲wood

Absolute Accommodation

HOW LUXURY WORKS

Some of the designs collected in this book call to mind the palatial estates of the Old World, where royal families found retreat from the rigors of life in court. And though you may not be royalty, you can still rely on your new home for the comfort and rejuvenation that contemporary life compels us to find.

THE ROYAL TREATMENT

Luxury living is about exceeding conventional expectations and attaining a highly customized level of convenience. Look for homes that deliver absolute accommodation for your style of living. Consider all the things about the layout of your current home that dissatisfy you and imagine how you'd change them.

For example, where would you prefer to have the main bedroom? Most layouts reserve the back of the home at either end of the plan for the master suite, where it can find the most privacy. Some home-owners, preferring not to climb stairs to retire at night or to start the day, also insist on a first-floor location for the master bedroom. One-story plans are popular exactly for this reason, among others. On the other hand, a multistory plan can mean a private balcony or bayed sitting nook with a vantage of an especially picturesque landscape. In that case, you may prefer a plan with an upstairs master and a second set of stairs or a built-in home elevator.

Introduction

ABOVE: A bath-side garden window can take advantage of outstanding views.
RIGHT: The Roman bath is a popular theme for high-end suites—and for good reason.

When considering the location of private spaces, think also about where the bulk of the home's leisure activities will take place. Large-scale formal entertaining will require a full-fledged dining room with convenient access to the kitchen and overflow to a living room or formalized great room. Alternately, a properly designed deck or lanai, preferably with a catering kitchen, can help greatly in the completion of an outdoor dinner or poolside gathering.

HOLDING COURT

Informal entertainment for the family will likely take place in the great room or game room. But more recent trends and products have allowed flexible, on-demand options for where the family finds its fun. For example, small media centers spread around the home—in the kitchen, in the bath, and within bedrooms—allow for spontaneous family gatherings and media breaks to complement movie nights in the home theater. Beyond mere entertainment, media centers enable the family to take care of online banking, messaging, and other household duties to be completed wherever you happen to be.

Redundant media centers are just one way to build technology into your new home. Called home automation, the coordination of household devices under a unified network can assist the homeowners in many ways. Home automation improves upon the functionality and convenience of devices you already depend on—televisions, smoke detectors, thermostats, speakers, security systems, and motion sensors—and allow them to work cooperatively.

For example, the door and window sensors of a typical home security system are triggered separately whenever monitored doors and windows open or close. The triggers are isolated events in a typical system and do not provide a more meaningful report of the home environment. By contrast, an integrated home automation system can distinguish between "motion sensor-triggered, window contact-triggered" (homeowner walks across room, opens window) and "window contact-triggered, motion sensor-triggered" (someone opens window, enters home). The first event has bearing on the temperature system, which would compensate by lowering the thermostat in the affected area of the home. The second event concerns the security system, which could notify the monitoring center about a possible break-in. To find out more about integrating home automation into your house plan, turn to page 187.

MAINTAIN THE DOMAIN

Even a luxury homeowner must deal with dishes, kids doing homework, and all the other chores of everyday life. That your family can enjoy their downtime during the day while evening guests marvel at your picture-perfect home is a reflection, then, of how hard you and your home must work to keep it well-presented.

Insist on amenities that keep unsightly piles and clutter under control. Laundry rooms should be able to perform related chores, such as dry cleaning, sewing and mending, and storage. A mudroom or similarly functioning "landing zone" should receive incoming traffic with individualized spaces for keys, wallets, briefcases, umbrellas, golf bags, and other carry-ons. In fact, children may appreciate lockers for sports equipment and pet gear. In bathrooms, adequate vanity storage is a must for keeping beauty products and personal appliances from running amok.

Do not attempt to keep boxes of seasonal items in a corner of the garage. Dedicate an air-conditioned room for the storage of holiday decorations, camping equipment, unused furniture, wine, and family archives. If the room can be additionally secured, it may be able to function as an aesthetically pleasing safe room or emergency shelter. Other specialized spaces—libraries, offices, meditation rooms, exercise rooms, art studios, private gardens—can truly personalize a home. Even if a plan does not mention a room you want, modify the plan to accommodate a custom-installed space. Remember that a house plan is just a starting place in the design of your home. Read more about plan modification on page 186.

ABOVE: A luxury home should be prepared with the space to serve myriad guests and visitors.
OPPOSITE: This three-season living area combines a kitchen, family room, fireplace, and outdoor elements to produce a beautiful entertaining space.

Introduction

Many specialized rooms, such as this wine cellar, find homes in the lower and upper levels of luxury designs.

RIGHT: The master suite is often the home's crown jewel. This one includes a sitting area and Mediterranean-themed details.
BELOW: Screened porches pale in comparison to Palladian-window-lit sunrooms. The two-story height really soars.

CROWNING ACHIEVEMENT

The luxury home's credo of absolute accommodation reaches its peak in the master bathroom, inspired by the pamper-till-you-drop promise of getaway resorts and spas. For few other places in the home will you find the same array of options and upgrades. Highest-end baths are bound to include a whirlpool or soaking tub, steam shower, sauna, and other "spa-meni-ties." Tubs should include hand-held sprayers, both for easy bathing and cleaning, and showers should include seating. In place of a traditional wall-mounted vanity counter, custom-fit furnishings and drawers establish a more elegant tone. First-floor baths can take advantage of the landscape by adding on a privacy garden; second-floor baths work well with a small balcony. As far as square footage goes, the larger the better: Work against the open-layout trend in the rest of the home by separating His and Her spaces, for closets, vanities, and toilets. For the truly fortunate, entirely separating the master baths will keep homeowners happily groomed. ∎

RIGHT: Two double-bay garages flank a center entry marked by Greek columns and a glass-and-wood door.
BELOW: Stone columns and arches create a rear deck accessed from the main-level breakfast nook.
OPPOSITE: Wrought iron spindles and designs on the front door and windows decorate the foyer. The pattern repeats above the doors in the hallway.

Greek Menagerie

INCORPORATING THE BEST OF EUROPEAN DESIGNS

A tribute to Greek architecture, the stucco, stone, and siding exterior fits well along the coast while its muted colors also let it blend in among hilltops. Partial pediments divide the rooftop in three symmetrical sections supported by Grecian columns in the forefront of a double hipped roof, which makes this home a true hybrid of Old World styles.

A coffered great room greets visitors upon entering through the center door of three arch-topped, artisan windows. To the left, beyond the dining room, a gourmet island kitchen shares space with a cozy hearth room. In turn, the hearth room shares the fireplace and surrounding built-ins with the adjacent great room. A nearby laundry room joins the home with the two-car garage.

PHOTOS BY AHMANN DESIGN, INC.

LEFT: The kitchen, with its snack-bar island and attached breakfast table, and the adjoining hearth room make this a convenient space for casual meals and entertaining.
BELOW: In the downstairs rec room, a curved bar stands guard in front of the wine cellar entrance.
OPPOSITE: The great room includes a wall of windows overlooking the rear property and a full-sized wall of carved wood and niches shared with the hearth room. A brick fireplace surround below the mantel gives a sense of history.

The right wing houses a den, the master suite, and a second two-car garage. The master bedroom's square shape and wall of windows provide space for furniture placement while allowing in plenty of natural light. Enter the master bath to find a separate corner shower and spa tub and double vanity preceding the enormous walk-in closet.

The lower level houses the entertainment rooms along with three family bedrooms. Work out in the private exercise room and store your finest vintage in the dedicated wine cellar. ■

European Luxury

ABOVE: Mosaic and geometric tiles on the master bath shower and tub, and columns that support a curved ceiling, contribute to the home's Greek style.
RIGHT: An aged, crackle finish on the headboard and footboard repeats in the tray ceiling above the master bedroom.

MAIN LEVEL

LOWER LEVEL

PLAN HPK2400001

MAIN LEVEL: 2,262 SQ. FT.
LOWER LEVEL: 2,195 SQ. FT.
TOTAL: 4,457 SQ. FT.
BEDROOMS: 4
BATHROOMS: 3½
WIDTH: 76' - 0"
DEPTH: 59' - 4"
FOUNDATION: Finished Basement

ORDER ONLINE @ EPLANS.COM

PLAN HPK2400002

FIRST FLOOR: 2,398 SQ. FT.
SECOND FLOOR: 657 SQ. FT.
TOTAL: 3,055 SQ. FT.
BONUS SPACE: 374 SQ. FT.
BEDROOMS: 4
BATHROOMS: 3½
WIDTH: 72' - 8"
DEPTH: 69' - 1"
FOUNDATION: CRAWLSPACE,
UNFINISHED BASEMENT

ORDER ONLINE @ EPLANS.COM

SECOND FLOOR

FIRST FLOOR

European formality meets a bold American spirit in this splendid plan. Perfect for a lake or golf course setting, this home offers walls of windows in the living areas. Soak up the scenery in the sunroom, which opens from the breakfast nook and leads to a rear terrace or deck. Ten-foot ceilings throughout the main level provide interior vistas and add volume to the rooms. The library features a tray ceiling and an arched window and would make an excellent home office or guest suite. Classical columns divide the great room and dining room, which has a see-through wet bar. The deluxe master suite uses defining columns between the bedroom and the lavish bath and walk-in closet. Upstairs, there are two additional suites and a bonus room.

HELPFUL HINT! Modify your plan with our easy-to-use customization service.

PLAN HPK2400003

First Floor: 1,583 sq. ft.

Second Floor: 1,632 sq. ft.

Total: 3,215 sq. ft.

Bedrooms: 5

Bathrooms: 4½

Width: 58' - 4"

Depth: 50' - 0"

Foundation: Crawlspace,
Unfinished Walkout Basement

ORDER ONLINE @ EPLANS.COM

From outside to inside, the decorative details on this stucco two-story make it very special. Ceiling adornments are particularly interesting: the two-story foyer and the master bedroom have tray ceilings. The dining room and living room are separated by columns; another column graces the two-story family room. A den is reached through double doors just to the left of the foyer. Use it for an additional bedroom if needed—it has a private bath. There are four upstairs bedrooms in this plan. The master suite includes a fireplace in the vaulted sitting room.

SECOND FLOOR

FIRST FLOOR

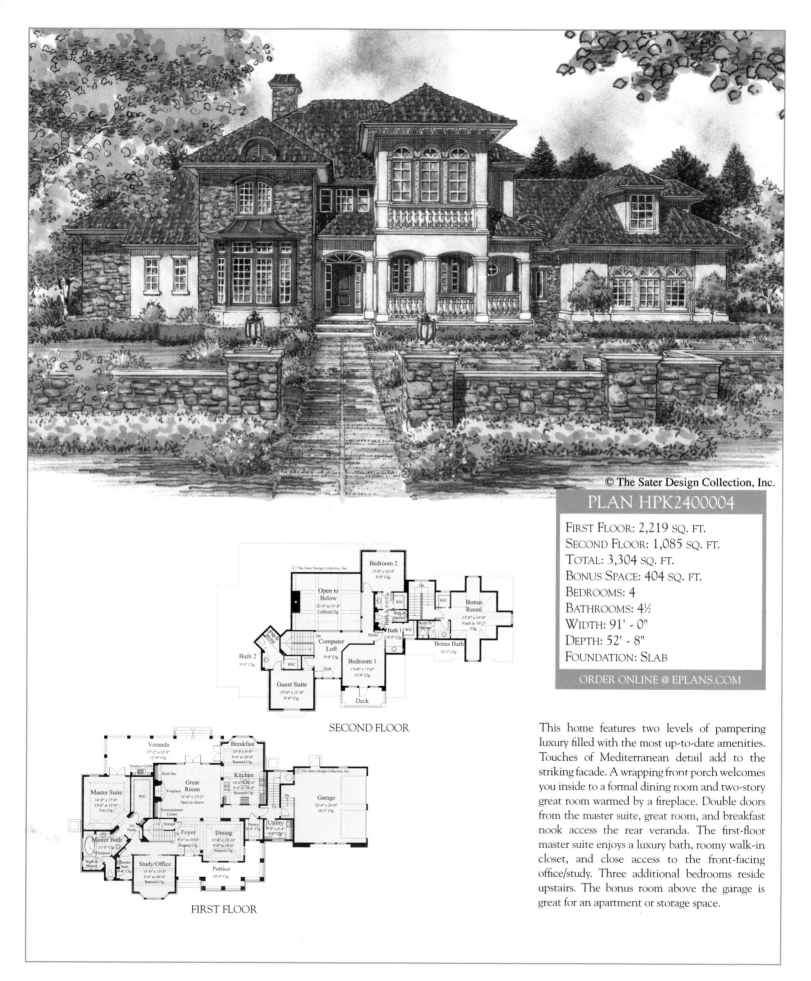

© The Sater Design Collection, Inc.

PLAN HPK2400004

FIRST FLOOR: 2,219 SQ. FT.
SECOND FLOOR: 1,085 SQ. FT.
TOTAL: 3,304 SQ. FT.
BONUS SPACE: 404 SQ. FT.
BEDROOMS: 4
BATHROOMS: 4½
WIDTH: 91' - 0"
DEPTH: 52' - 8"
FOUNDATION: SLAB

ORDER ONLINE @ EPLANS.COM

SECOND FLOOR

FIRST FLOOR

This home features two levels of pampering luxury filled with the most up-to-date amenities. Touches of Mediterranean detail add to the striking facade. A wrapping front porch welcomes you inside to a formal dining room and two-story great room warmed by a fireplace. Double doors from the master suite, great room, and breakfast nook access the rear veranda. The first-floor master suite enjoys a luxury bath, roomy walk-in closet, and close access to the front-facing office/study. Three additional bedrooms reside upstairs. The bonus room above the garage is great for an apartment or storage space.

PLAN HPK2400005

FIRST FLOOR: 2,898 SQ. FT.
SECOND FLOOR: 441 SQ. FT.
TOTAL: 3,339 SQ. FT.
BEDROOMS: 4
BATHROOMS: 4
WIDTH: 80' - 0"
DEPTH: 67' - 0"
FOUNDATION: SLAB

ORDER ONLINE @ EPLANS.COM

Essentially a one-story home, the bulk of the amenities can be found on the first floor. The kitchen and breakfast area adjoin the family room, which leads to two of the four bedrooms. On the opposite side of the plan, the roomy master suite offers two walk-in closets, a garden tub, a separate shower, dual vanities, and access to the covered patio. The second story houses the fourth family bedroom complete with a full bath and a walk-in closet. A side-loading three-car garage adds appeal.

SECOND FLOOR

FIRST FLOOR

PHOTOGRAPHY BY MARK ENGLUND/HOMESTORE PLANS & PUBLICATIONS

ORDER blueprints anytime at 1-800-521-6797 or eplans.com

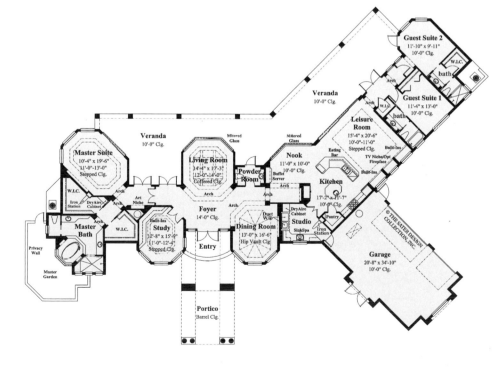

PLAN HPK2400006

SQUARE FOOTAGE: 3,398
BEDROOMS: 3
BATHROOMS: 3½
WIDTH: 121' - 5"
DEPTH: 96' - 2"
FOUNDATION: SLAB

ORDER ONLINE @ EPLANS.COM

Bringing the outdoors in through a multitude of bay windows is what this design is all about. The grand foyer opens to the living room with a magnificent view to the covered lanai. The study and dining room flank the foyer. The master suite is found on the left with an opulent private bath and views of the private garden. To the right, the kitchen adjoins the nook that boasts a mitered-glass bay window overlooking the lanai. Beyond the leisure room are two guest rooms, each with private baths.

PLAN HPK2400007

Square Footage: 3,477
Bedrooms: 3
Bathrooms: 3½
Width: 95' - 0"
Depth: 88' - 8"
Foundation: Slab

ORDER ONLINE @ EPLANS.COM

Make dreams come true with this fine, sunny design. An octagonal study provides a nice focal point both inside and out. The living areas remain open to each other and access outdoor areas. A wet bar makes entertaining a breeze, especially with a window pass-through to a grill area on the lanai. The kitchen shares space with a lovely breakfast nook and a bright leisure room. Two bedrooms are located near the family living center. In the master bedroom suite, luxury abounds with a two-way fireplace, a morning kitchen, two walk-in closets, and a compartmented bath. Another full bath accommodates a pool area.

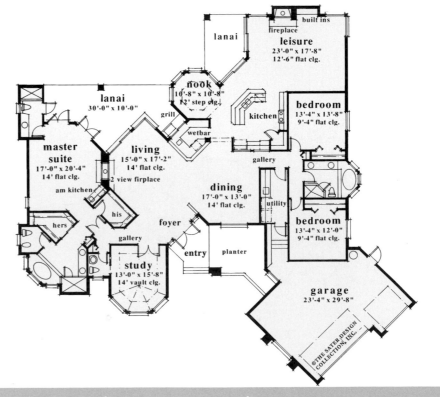

Helpful Hint! Reproducible plans are your best value. You can make as many copies as you need!

PLAN HPK2400008

First Floor: 2,658 sq. ft.
Second Floor: 854 sq. ft.
Total: 3,512 sq. ft.
Bonus Space: 150 sq. ft.
Bedrooms: 4
Bathrooms: 3½
Width: 86' - 0"
Depth: 58' - 1"
Foundation: Crawlspace, Slab,
Unfinished Basement

ORDER ONLINE @ EPLANS.COM

SECOND FLOOR

FIRST FLOOR

This grand country estate presents an impressive exterior of brick and fieldstone with a hooded bay window as the focal point. This two-story design features a magnificent curved staircase from the foyer to the second level. A secluded study and formal dining room are at the front of the house. The master bedroom suite features a unique curved vanity and oversized twin walk-in closets. The main living areas are connected by a tiled gallery. One family bedroom suite is on the first level; two additional bedrooms and full bath share the second level with a playroom and a large bonus room with access to attic storage.

PLAN HPK2400009

FIRST FLOOR: 1,786 SQ. FT.
SECOND FLOOR: 1,739 SQ. FT.
TOTAL: 3,525 SQ. FT.
BEDROOMS: 5
BATHROOMS: 4½
WIDTH: 59' - 0"
DEPTH: 53' - 0"
FOUNDATION: CRAWLSPACE, SLAB,
UNFINISHED WALKOUT BASEMENT

ORDER ONLINE @ EPLANS.COM

European details bring charm and a touch of joie de vivre to this traditional home. Casual living space includes a two-story family room with a centered fireplace. A sizable kitchen, with an island serving bar and a French door to the rear property, leads to the formal dining room through a convenient butler's pantry. The second floor includes a generous master suite with a sitting room defined by decorative columns and five lovely windows. Bedroom 2 has a private bath, and two additional bedrooms share a hall bath with compartmented lavatories.

SECOND FLOOR

FIRST FLOOR

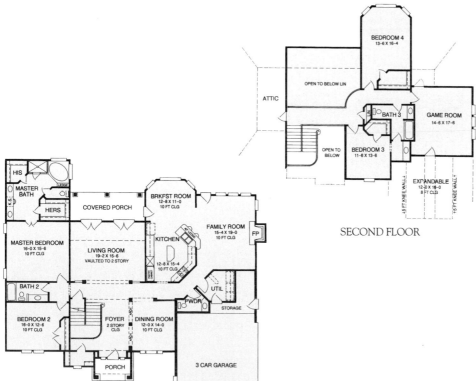

SECOND FLOOR

FIRST FLOOR

PLAN HPK2400010

FIRST FLOOR: 2,518 SQ. FT.
SECOND FLOOR: 1,013 SQ. FT.
TOTAL: 3,531 SQ. FT.
BONUS SPACE: 192 SQ. FT.
BEDROOMS: 4
BATHROOMS: 3½
WIDTH: 67' - 8"
DEPTH: 74' - 2"
FOUNDATION: CRAWLSPACE, SLAB,
UNFINISHED BASEMENT

ORDER ONLINE @ EPLANS.COM

Old World charm gives this design its universal appeal. The mixture of stone and brick on the exterior elevation gives the home a warm, inviting feel. Inside, an up-to-date floor plan has it all. Two living areas provide space for both formal and informal entertaining. The kitchen and breakfast room are open to the large family room. The master suite and a secondary bedroom are located on the first floor. The second bedroom makes a great nursery, study, or convenient guest bedroom. Upstairs, Bedrooms 3 and 4 share a large bath including private dressing areas.

PLAN HPK2400011

First Floor: 2,384 sq. ft.
Second Floor: 1,234 sq. ft.
Total: 3,618 sq. ft.
Bonus Space: 344 sq. ft.
Bedrooms: 5
Bathrooms: 4½
Width: 64' - 6"
Depth: 57' - 10"
Foundation: Crawlspace, Slab,
Unfinished Walkout Basement

ORDER ONLINE @ EPLANS.COM

Stucco and stone, French shutters, a turret-style bay, and lovely arches create a magical, timeless style. A formal arch romanticizes the front entry, which opens to a two-story foyer. A bayed living room resides to the right, and a formal dining room is set to the left. Straight ahead, the vaulted two-story family room is warmed by an enchanting fireplace. The island kitchen is set between the breakfast and dining rooms. The master suite is enhanced by a tray ceiling and offers a lavish master bath with a whirlpool tub. Upstairs, Bedroom 2 offers another private bath and a walk-in closet. Bedrooms 3 and 4 each provide their own walk-in closets and share a full bath. The bonus room is perfect for a future home office or playroom.

SECOND FLOOR

FIRST FLOOR

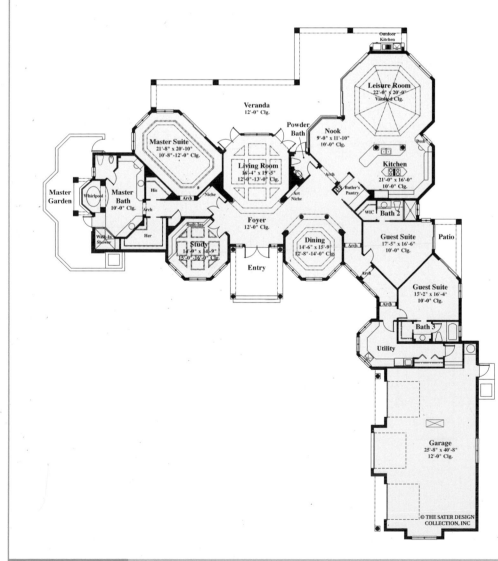

© The Sater Design Collection, Inc

REAR EXTERIOR

PLAN HPK2400012

SQUARE FOOTAGE: 3,688
BEDROOMS: 3
BATHROOMS: 3½
WIDTH: 129' - 0"
DEPTH: 102' - 0"
FOUNDATION: Slab

ORDER ONLINE @ EPLANS.COM

Perfect for the California coast, this stucco design is an alluring masterpiece. The luxurious interior is introduced by a set of double doors that open into the spacious foyer. The foyer is flanked on either side by the study and exquisite dining room shaped by elegant columns. Straight ahead, the formal living room opens through two sets of double doors onto a rear terrace. The gourmet island kitchen overlooks the tiled nook and leisure room. An outdoor kitchen conveniently serves the pool area, which features a cozy spa and cascading spillover. The master suite indulges with enchanting style. Walk past two walk-in closets to the spacious master bath with whirlpool tub luxury. A door from the master bath accesses a private side garden. Two guest suites on the opposite side of the home share a full bath off the utility room. A three-car garage completes this plan.

HELPFUL HINT! Typical home construction requires 8 to 12 copies of your plan.

© The Sater Design Collection, Inc.

PLAN HPK2400013

SQUARE FOOTAGE: 3,743
BEDROOMS: 4
BATHROOMS: 3½
WIDTH: 80' - 0"
DEPTH: 103' - 8"
FOUNDATION: SLAB

ORDER ONLINE @ EPLANS.COM

With California style and Mediterranean good looks, this striking stucco manor is sure to delight. The portico and foyer open to reveal a smart plan with convenience and flexibility in mind. The columned living room has a warming fireplace and access to the rear property. In the gourmet kitchen, an open design with an island and walk-in pantry will please any chef. From here, the elegant dining room and sunny nook are easily served. The leisure room is separated from the game room by a built-in entertainment center. The game area can also be finished off as a bedroom. To the rear, a guest room is perfect for frequent visitors or as an in-law suite. The master suite features a bright sitting area, oversized walk-in closets, and a pampering bath with a whirlpool tub. Extra features not to be missed: the outdoor grill, game-room storage, and gallery window seat.

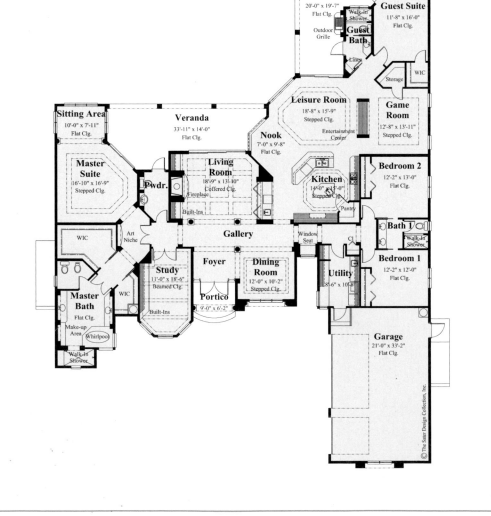

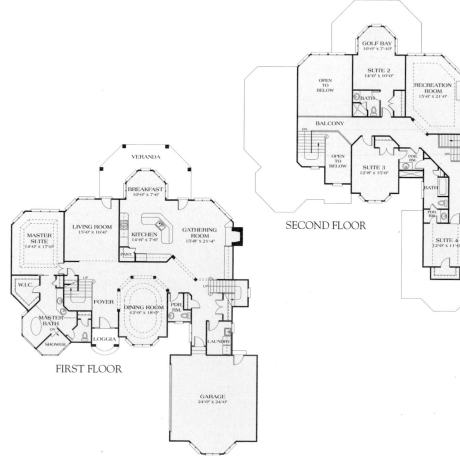

SECOND FLOOR

FIRST FLOOR

PLAN HPK2400014

FIRST FLOOR: 2,292 SQ. FT.
SECOND FLOOR: 1,465 SQ. FT.
TOTAL: 3,757 SQ. FT.
BEDROOMS: 4
BATHROOMS: 3½
WIDTH: 67' - 6"
DEPTH: 78' - 0"
FOUNDATION: CRAWLSPACE

ORDER ONLINE @ EPLANS.COM

An illusion of softness is projected by the arches, circles, bays, and bows of this unique four-bedroom contemporary home. Graceful columns define the dining room with its oval tray ceiling and bay window and the entrance to the gathering room that includes a fireplace and access to the covered veranda. An island kitchen is open to a five-sided breakfast nook with windows facing the veranda. Glass-block windows enclose the master bath and shower and the master bedroom features a tray ceiling. A balcony on the second floor connects three additional bedroom suites and a large recreation room with fireplace.

PLAN HPK2400015

SQUARE FOOTAGE: 3,877
BEDROOMS: 3
BATHROOMS: 3½
WIDTH: 102' - 4"
DEPTH: 98' - 10"
FOUNDATION: SLAB

ORDER ONLINE @ EPLANS.COM

Simple yet stunning, this home proves that you can have it all: beauty and elegance in an at-home environment. At the entry, arched transoms allow sunlight into the foyer and the living room. To the left of the living room is the dining area with a tray ceiling and French doors that open to the veranda. To the right, a see-through fireplace is shared with the study. Wrapping counters, a corner pantry, and an island in the gourmet kitchen allow stress-free meal preparation. The leisure room opens to the spacious morning nook, displays a pyramid ceiling, and includes a warming fireplace. The master suite greets homeowners with lovely French doors and provides access to a master bath with a whirlpool tub, separate shower, two vanities, and a walk-in closet.

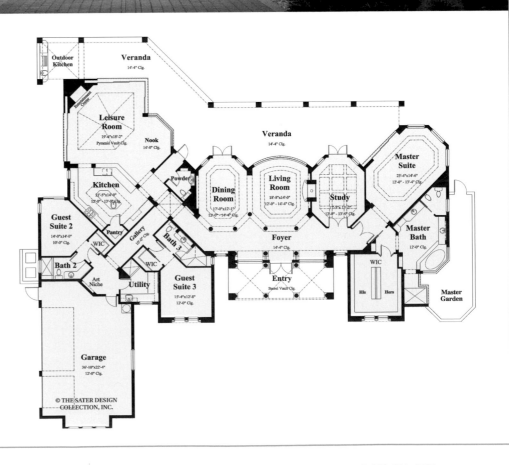

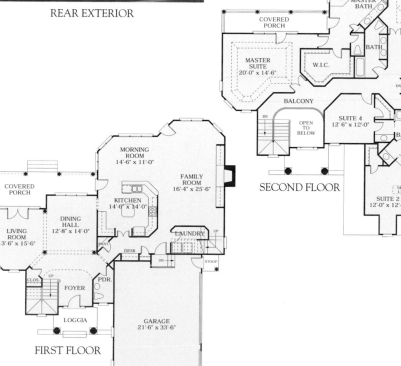

REAR EXTERIOR

PLAN HPK2400016

FIRST FLOOR: 1,741 SQ. FT.
SECOND FLOOR: 2,141 SQ. FT.
TOTAL: 3,882 SQ. FT.
BEDROOMS: 4
BATHROOMS: 3½
WIDTH: 61' - 8"
DEPTH: 69' - 6"
FOUNDATION: CRAWLSPACE

ORDER ONLINE @ EPLANS.COM

The grand, elegant entry of this classic French country design reflects the unusual floor plan inside. A wide foyer with powder room and guest closet opens directly into the formal dining room flanked by columns. The living room to the left features angled windows and double doors leading to a covered porch. The family room, morning room and island kitchen all flow together and are highlighted by a fireplace and built-in bookcases. The master bedroom suite on the second floor opens onto a private covered porch. Three additional bedrooms with two baths, plus a large bonus room complete the second level.

SECOND FLOOR

FIRST FLOOR

© The Sater Design Collection, Inc.

PLAN HPK2400017

SQUARE FOOTAGE: 3,942
BEDROOMS: 3
BATHROOMS: 4
WIDTH: 83' - 10"
DEPTH: 106' - 0"
FOUNDATION: SLAB

ORDER ONLINE @ EPLANS.COM

Welcome home to a country manor with Renaissance flair. Full-length, squint-style windows and brick accents bring Old World charm to a modern plan. Designed for flexibility, the open foyer, living room, and dining room have infinite decor options. Down a gallery (with art niches), two bedroom suites enjoy private baths. The bon-vivant island kitchen is introduced with a wet bar and pool bath. In the leisure room, family and friends will revel in expansive views of the rear property. An outdoor kitchen on the lanai invites alfresco dining. Separated for ultimate privacy, the master suite is an exercise in luxurious living. Past the morning kitchen and into the grand bedroom, an octagonal sitting area is bathed in light. The bath is gracefully set in the turret, with a whirlpool tub and views of the master garden.

HELPFUL HINT!   Remember: You'll need copies of your plan for your builder, contractors, building department, and you!

32   Order blueprints anytime at 1-800-521-6797 or eplans.com

© The Sater Design Collection, Inc.

SECOND FLOOR

FIRST FLOOR

© The Sater Design Collection, Inc.

PLAN HPK2400018

FIRST FLOOR: 2,834 SQ. FT.

SECOND FLOOR: 1,143 SQ. FT.

TOTAL: 3,977 SQ. FT.

BEDROOMS: 4

BATHROOMS: 3½

WIDTH: 85' - 0"

DEPTH: 76' - 8"

FOUNDATION: Slab

ORDER ONLINE @ EPLANS.COM

Mediterranean accents enhance the facade of this contemporary estate home. Two fanciful turret bays add a sense of grandeur to the exterior. Double doors open inside to a grand two-story foyer. A two-sided fireplace warms the study and living room, with a two-story coffered ceiling. To the right, the master suite includes a private bath, two walk-in closets, and double-door access to the sweeping rear veranda. Casual areas of the home include the gourmet island kitchen, breakfast nook, and leisure room warmed by a fireplace. A spiral staircase leads upstairs, where a second-floor balcony separates two family bedrooms from the luxurious guest suite.

© The Sater Design Collection, Inc.

PLAN HPK2400019

First Floor: 2,850 sq. ft.
Second Floor: 1,155 sq. ft.
Total: 4,005 sq. ft.
Bonus Space: 371 sq. ft.
Bedrooms: 4
Bathrooms: 4½
Width: 71' - 6"
Depth: 83' - 0"
Foundation: Slab

ORDER ONLINE @ EPLANS.COM

Stone, stucco, and soaring rooflines combine to give this elegant Mediterranean design a stunning exterior. The interior is packed with luxurious amenities, from the wall of glass in the living room to the whirlpool tub in the master bath. A dining room and study serve as formal areas, while a leisure room with a fireplace offers a relaxing retreat. The first-floor master suite boasts a private bayed sitting area. Upstairs, all three bedrooms include private baths; Bedroom 2 and the guest suite also provide walk-in closets.

SECOND FLOOR

FIRST FLOOR

PLAN HPK2400020

First Floor: 2,608 sq. ft.
Second Floor: 1,432 sq. ft.
Total: 4,040 sq. ft.
Bedrooms: 4
Bathrooms: 3½
Width: 89' - 10"
Depth: 63' - 8"
Foundation: Crawlspace, Slab

ORDER ONLINE @ EPLANS.COM

SECOND FLOOR

FIRST FLOOR

A distinctively French flair is the hallmark of this European design. Inside, the two-story foyer provides views to the huge great room beyond. A well-placed study off the foyer provides space for a home office. The kitchen, breakfast room, and sunroom are adjacent and lend a spacious feel. The great room is visible from this area through decorative arches. The master suite includes a roomy sitting area and a lovely bath with a centerpiece whirlpool tub flanked by half-columns. Upstairs, Bedrooms 2 and 3 share a bath that includes separate dressing areas.

PLAN HPK2400021

First Floor: 2,095 sq. ft.
Second Floor: 1,954 sq. ft.
Total: 4,049 sq. ft.
Bedrooms: 5
Bathrooms: 4½
Width: 56' - 0"
Depth: 63' - 0"
Foundation: Crawlspace,
Unfinished Walkout Basement

ORDER ONLINE @ EPLANS.COM

The French Country facade of this lovely design hints at the enchanting amenities found within. A two-story foyer welcomes you inside. To the right, a bayed living room is separated from the formal dining room by graceful columns. A butler's pantry leads to the gourmet island kitchen. The breakfast room accesses a rear covered porch and shares a casual area with the two-story family room. Here, a fireplace flanked by built-ins adds to the relaxing atmosphere. Bedroom 5, with a private bath, converts to an optional study. Upstairs, the master suite offers palatial elegance. Here, the sitting room is warmed by a fireplace flanked by built-ins and the suite accesses a private second-floor porch. A dressing room leads to the vaulted master bath and enormous His and Hers walk-in closets. Three additional bedrooms are available on the second floor.

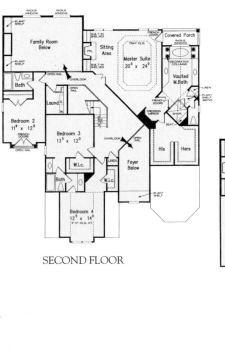

SECOND FLOOR

FIRST FLOOR

Order blueprints anytime at 1-800-521-6797 or eplans.com

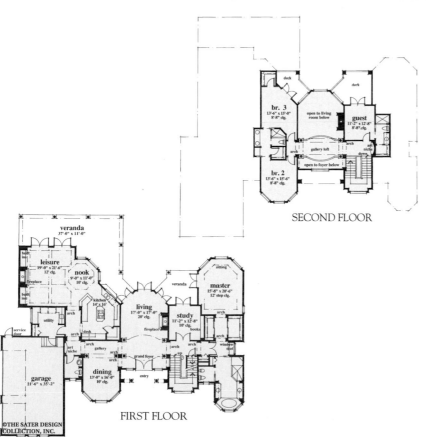

FIRST FLOOR

© THE SATER DESIGN COLLECTION, INC.

SECOND FLOOR

PLAN HPK2400022

FIRST FLOOR: 3,027 SQ. FT.
SECOND FLOOR: 1,079 SQ. FT.
TOTAL: 4,106 SQ. FT.
BEDROOMS: 4
BATHROOMS: 3½
WIDTH: 87' - 4"
DEPTH: 80' - 4"
FOUNDATION: UNFINISHED
BASEMENT

ORDER ONLINE @ EPLANS.COM

The inside of this design is just as majestic as the outside. The grand foyer opens to a two-story living room with a fireplace and magnificent views. Dining in the bayed formal dining room will be a memorable experience. A well-designed kitchen is near a sunny nook and a leisure room with a fireplace and outdoor access. The master wing includes a separate study and an elegant private bath. The second level features a guest suite with its own bath and deck, two family bedrooms (Bedroom 3 also has its own deck), and a gallery loft with views to the living room below.

PLAN HPK2400023

First Floor: 3,734 sq. ft.
Second Floor: 418 sq. ft.
Total: 4,152 sq. ft.
Bedrooms: 3
Bathrooms: 4½
Width: 82' - 0"
Depth: 107' - 8"
Foundation: Slab

ORDER ONLINE @ EPLANS.COM

Softly angled turrets add sweet drama to this dreamy Mediterranean manor, as a rambling interior plays function to everyday life. Beautiful interior columns in the foyer offer a fine introduction to open, spacious rooms. A secluded master suite features a beautiful bay window, a coffered ceiling, and French doors to the lanai. Across the master foyer, the private bath satisfies the homeowners' needs by offering a whirlpool tub, separate shower, private vanities, and two walk-in closets. Bedroom 2 includes a sitting bay, a walk-in closet, and a private bath. Upstairs, a spacious loft offers room for computers and books. A wet bar, walk-in closet, and full bath with a shower provide the possibility of converting this area to a bedroom suite.

SECOND FLOOR

FIRST FLOOR

PLAN HPK2400024

FIRST FLOOR: 2,547 SQ. FT.
SECOND FLOOR: 1,637 SQ. FT.
TOTAL: 4,184 SQ. FT.
BONUS SPACE: 802 SQ. FT.
BEDROOMS: 4
BATHROOMS: 3½
WIDTH: 74' - 0"
DEPTH: 95' - 6"
FOUNDATION: CRAWLSPACE

ORDER ONLINE @ EPLANS.COM

SECOND FLOOR

FIRST FLOOR

Double columns flank a raised loggia that leads to a beautiful two-story foyer. Flanking this elegance to the right is a formal dining room. Straight ahead, under a balcony and defined by yet more pillars, is the spacious grand room. A bow-windowed morning room and a gathering room feature a full view of the rear lanai and beyond. The master bedroom suite is lavish with its amenities, which include a bayed sitting area, direct access to the rear terrace, a walk-in closet, and a sumptuous bath.

PLAN HPK2400025

SQUARE FOOTAGE: 4,255
BEDROOMS: 3
BATHROOMS: 3½
WIDTH: 91' - 6"
DEPTH: 116' - 11"
FOUNDATION: SLAB

ORDER ONLINE @ EPLANS.COM

REAR EXTERIOR

This European stucco exterior provides great curb appeal and conceals a thoroughly modern arrangement of public and private rooms. A dramatic arched entry announces an open foyer that offers interior vistas and outdoor views through the formal rooms. A mitered wall of glass and a vaulted ceiling in the living room provide a spectacular introduction to this grand manor. The kitchen connects to the dining room through a butler's pantry. French doors lead from a central gallery to the master wing. The suite provides a sitting bay, lanai access, a soaking tub, and a compartmented toilet. Nearby, French doors lead to a study that converts to a library or office. Retreating glass walls connect the formal rooms to an area of the lanai that serves as an entertainment terrace.

© LAURENCE TAYLOR PHOTOGRAPHY

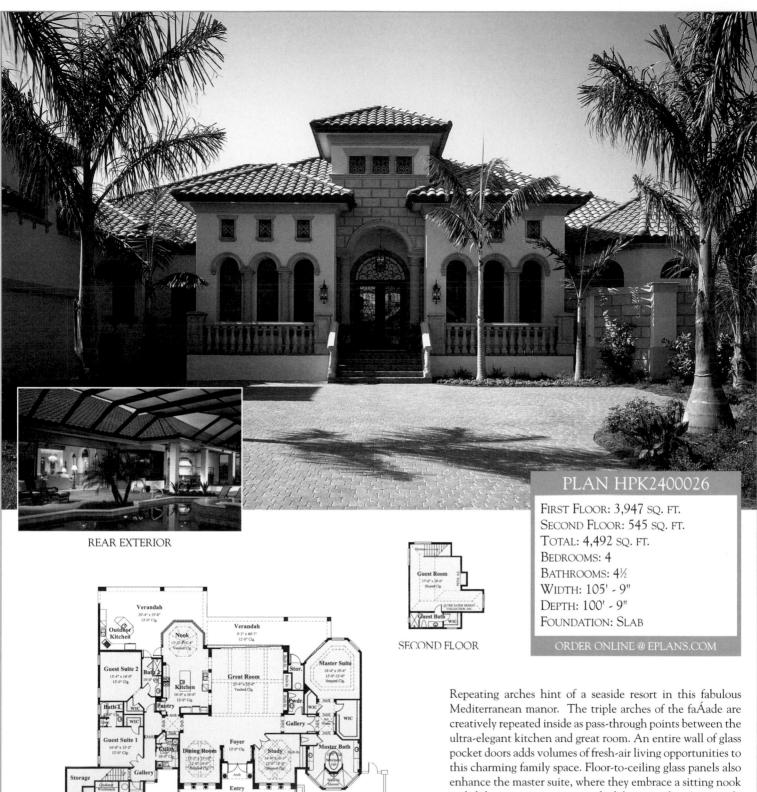

REAR EXTERIOR

SECOND FLOOR

FIRST FLOOR

PLAN HPK2400026

FIRST FLOOR: 3,947 SQ. FT.
SECOND FLOOR: 545 SQ. FT.
TOTAL: 4,492 SQ. FT.
BEDROOMS: 4
BATHROOMS: 4½
WIDTH: 105' - 9"
DEPTH: 100' - 9"
FOUNDATION: Slab

ORDER ONLINE @ EPLANS.COM

Repeating arches hint of a seaside resort in this fabulous Mediterranean manor. The triple arches of the faÁade are creatively repeated inside as pass-through points between the ultra-elegant kitchen and great room. An entire wall of glass pocket doors adds volumes of fresh-air living opportunities to this charming family space. Floor-to-ceiling glass panels also enhance the master suite, where they embrace a sitting nook and slide open to a private end of the veranda. A spa-style tub sits center stage in the master bath. Behind the curved wall is a walk-in shower with views to a private garden. The idyllic courtyard—with its stunning stone fireplace and gazebo-style, open-beamed canopy—has an arbor-like ambience perfect for a cool drink and warm friends. A twilight glow highlights the indoor-outdoor connections of this home as the public and private rooms cast their personalities outside to the meandering veranda and glittering pool.

REAR EXTERIOR

PLAN HPK2400027

FIRST FLOOR: 3,947 SQ. FT.
SECOND FLOOR: 545 SQ. FT.
TOTAL: 4,492 SQ. FT.
BEDROOMS: 4
BATHROOMS: 4½
WIDTH: 105' - 9"
DEPTH: 100' - 9"
FOUNDATION: SLAB

ORDER ONLINE @ EPLANS.COM

SECOND FLOOR

FIRST FLOOR

The Mediterranean appeal is undeniable and this home is no exception. The stucco exterior is accentuated by a red tile roof lending a timeless feel. The open floor plan and expansive outdoor living space is ideal for entertaining. The large rear veranda features an outdoor kitchen, perfect for alfresco meals. For more intimate occasions, relax in the private garden outside of the master bath.

HELPFUL HINT! Unlike plans from some other companies, each of our plans includes a full electrical schematic.

REAR EXTERIOR

PLAN HPK2400028

FIRST FLOOR: 3,478 SQ. FT.
SECOND FLOOR: 1,037 SQ. FT.
TOTAL: 4,515 SQ. FT.
BONUS SPACE: 314 SQ. FT.
BEDROOMS: 4
BATHROOMS: 4½
WIDTH: 86' - 8"
DEPTH: 84' - 4"
FOUNDATION: SLAB

ORDER ONLINE @ EPLANS.COM

SECOND FLOOR

FIRST FLOOR

Live it up in stunning Mediterranean style! This stucco beauty is accented by arched windows and a clay tiled roof. Inside, the living space goes on and on. The formal dining room flows into the center living room, where a double-sided fireplace also warms the kitchen and breakfast nook to the left. The island kitchen opens to the spacious hearth-warmed family room. A bedroom with a private patio is tucked to the left rear, convenient to a full bath and the laundry room. A hallway here accesses the three-car garage. On the opposite side of the plan, past the den/study, is the spectacular master suite. This suite pushes the limits of luxury with double walk-in closets, a bay window, and an enormous bath with a corner windowed tub and separate vanities. The second floor is home to two more bedrooms—each with its own bath—and a loft that opens to a balcony. Bonus space on this floor awaits expansion.

PLAN HPK2400029

First Floor: 3,739 sq. ft.
Second Floor: 778 sq. ft.
Total: 4,517 sq. ft.
Bedrooms: 4
Bathrooms: 5½ + ½
Width: 105' - 0"
Depth: 84' - 0"
Foundation: Slab

ORDER ONLINE @ EPLANS.COM

SECOND FLOOR

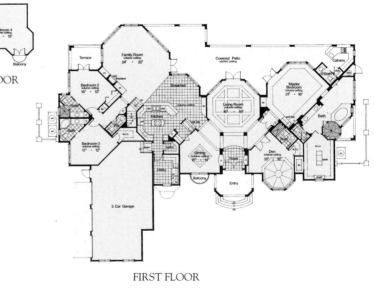

FIRST FLOOR

This estate embraces the style of southern France. Double doors open to a formal columned foyer and give views of the octagonal living room beyond. To the left is the formal dining room that connects to the kitchen via a butler's pantry. To the right is an unusual den with octagonal reading space. The master wing is immense. It features a wet bar, a private garden, and an exercise area. Two secondary bedrooms have private baths; Bedroom 2 has a private terrace. An additional bedroom with a private bath resides on the second floor, making it a perfect student's retreat. Also on the second floor is a game loft and storage area.

© Larry E. Belk Designs

SECOND FLOOR

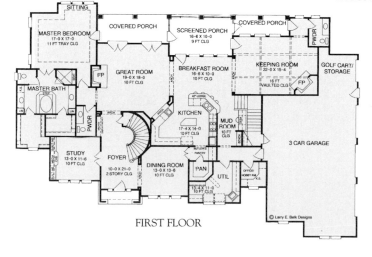

FIRST FLOOR

PLAN HPK2400030

FIRST FLOOR: 3,033 SQ. FT.
SECOND FLOOR: 1,545 SQ. FT.
TOTAL: 4,578 SQ. FT.
BEDROOMS: 4
BATHROOMS: 3½ + ½
WIDTH: 91' - 6"
DEPTH: 63' - 8"
FOUNDATION: CRAWLSPACE, SLAB,
UNFINISHED BASEMENT

ORDER ONLINE @ EPLANS.COM

This majestic storybook cottage, from the magical setting of rural Europe, provides the perfect home for any large family—with a wealth of modern comforts within. A graceful staircase cascades from the two-story foyer. To the left, a sophisticated study offers a wall of built-ins. To the right, a formal dining room is easily served from the island kitchen. The breakfast room accesses the rear screened porch. Fireplaces warm the great room and keeping room. Two sets of double doors open from the great room to the rear covered porch. The master bedroom features private porch access, a sitting area, lavish bath, and two walk-in closets. Upstairs, three additional family bedrooms offer walk-in closet space galore! The game room is great entertainment for both family and friends. A three-car garage with golf-cart storage completes the plan.

PLAN HPK2400031

First Floor: 3,933 sq. ft.
Second Floor: 719 sq. ft.
Total: 4,652 sq. ft.
Bedrooms: 4
Bathrooms: 4½
Width: 91' - 4"
Depth: 109' - 0"
Foundation: Slab

ORDER ONLINE @ EPLANS.COM

Beautiful and spacious, the artful disposition of this luxurious villa has a distinctly Mediterranean flavor. Dramatic and inspiring, the vaulted entry is set off by a dashing arch framed by columns, a barrel ceiling, and double doors that open to an expansive interior. The octagonal living room provides a fireplace and opens through two sets of lovely doors to the rear lanai. The master wing is a sumptuous retreat with double doors that open from a private vaulted foyer. One of the spacious guest suites can easily convert to personal quarters for a live-in relative. Another guest suite boasts a full bath, a bay window, and a walk-in closet. An upper-level loft leads to a third guest suite.

SECOND FLOOR

FIRST FLOOR

REAR EXTERIOR

PLAN HPK2400032

SQUARE FOOTAGE: 5,109
BEDROOMS: 4
BATHROOMS: 4½
WIDTH: 100' - 0"
DEPTH: 138' - 10"
FOUNDATION: SLAB

ORDER ONLINE @ EPLANS.COM

This Mediterranean palace is the home of your dreams! Whether you've been fantasizing about impressive spaces in which to entertain your friends, or luxurious privacy to while away your leisure time, this home has it all. An outdoor barbecue may take place on the exotic lanai, which spans the back of the home with access from the leisure room, the master suite, and the guest room. A more intimate solana to the side of the home provides a place to retreat by the fire as the night air settles in. In cooler weather, entertain in the formal living and dining rooms, complete with convenient wet bar and wine cooler. When the party is over, retreat to the master suite, which occupies an entire wing of the home. Don't miss the master spa, where you can bathe in a private garden!

HELPFUL HINT! Our custom modification service can add a walk-out basement to any plan—great for hillside lots!

REAR EXTERIOR

PLAN HPK2400033

First Floor: 3,307 sq. ft.
Second Floor: 2,015 sq. ft.
Total: 5,322 sq. ft.
Bonus Space: 373 sq. ft.
Bedrooms: 5
Bathrooms: 5½ + ½
Width: 143' - 3"
Depth: 71' - 2"
Foundation: Crawlspace

ORDER ONLINE @ EPLANS.COM

SECOND FLOOR

FIRST FLOOR

You'll be amazed at what this estate has to offer. A study/parlor and a formal dining room announce a grand foyer. Ahead, the living room offers a wet bar and French doors to the rear property. The kitchen is dazzling, with an enormous pantry, oversized cooktop island ... even a pizza oven! The gathering room has a corner fireplace and accesses the covered veranda. To the far right, the master suite is a delicious retreat from the world. A bowed window lets in light and a romantic fireplace makes chilly nights cozy. The luxurious bath is awe-inspiring, with a Roman tub and separate compartmented toilet areas—one with a bidet. Upstairs, three family bedrooms share a generous bonus room. A separate pool house is available, which includes a fireplace, full bath, and dressing area.

PHOTO BY ROBERT BAILEY, PHOTO COURTESY OF LIVING CONCEPTS HOME

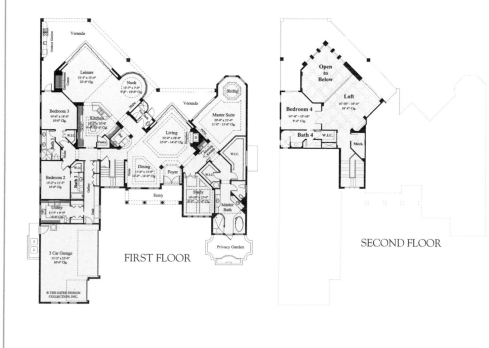

REAR EXTERIOR

PLAN HPK2400034

FIRST FLOOR: 4,137 SQ. FT.
SECOND FLOOR: 876 SQ. FT.
TOTAL: 5,013 SQ. FT.
BEDROOMS: 4
BATHROOMS: 5
WIDTH: 81' - 10"
DEPTH: 113' - 0"
FOUNDATION: SLAB

ORDER ONLINE @ EPLANS.COM

FIRST FLOOR

SECOND FLOOR

Decorative columns grace the entrance of this majestic estate, adding elegance and allure to an already impressive facade. Inside, the open layout lends itself to entertaining with the living and dining rooms centrally located, adjacent to a wet bar. The master suite dominates the right side of the plan, complete with a sitting room and privacy garden and replete with upgraded amenities, including a morning kitchen. The spacious study is conveniently located nearby. Boasting a built-in entertainment center, the leisure room at the rear of the home will be a family favorite. An outdoor kitchen on the veranda makes alfresco meals an option. The second floor houses a bedroom, full bath, and loft—perfect for guests.

© Larry E. Belk Designs

PLAN HPK2400035

First Floor: 3,058 sq. ft.
Second Floor: 2,076 sq. ft.
Total: 5,134 sq. ft.
Bedrooms: 4
Bathrooms: 4½
Width: 79' - 6"
Depth: 73' - 10"
Foundation: Crawlspace, Slab,
Unfinished Basement

ORDER ONLINE @ EPLANS.COM

This sweeping European facade, featuring a majestic turret-style bay, will easily be a stand-out in the neighborhood and a family favorite. The foyer opens to a spacious formal receiving area. Double doors from the living room open to the rear porch for outdoor activities. The master wing features a sitting area, a luxurious master bath, and two walk-in closets. The spacious island kitchen works with the bayed breakfast for more intimate meals. The family room offers a warm and relaxing fireplace. A private raised study, three-car garage, and utility room complete the first floor. Upstairs, three additional family bedrooms share the second floor with a music loft, hobby room, and game room.

SECOND FLOOR

FIRST FLOOR

REAR EXTERIOR

SECOND FLOOR

FIRST FLOOR

PLAN HPK2400036

FIRST FLOOR: 3,520 SQ. FT.
SECOND FLOOR: 1,638 SQ. FT.
TOTAL: 5,158 SQ. FT.
BONUS SPACE: 411 SQ. FT.
BEDROOMS: 5
BATHROOMS: 4½
WIDTH: 96' - 6"
DEPTH: 58' - 8"

ORDER ONLINE @ EPLANS.COM

This custom-designed estate home elegantly combines stone and stucco, arched windows, and stunning exterior details under its formidable hipped roof. The two-story foyer is impressive with its grand staircase, tray ceiling, and overlooking balcony. Equally remarkable is the generous living room with a fireplace and a coffered two-story ceiling. The kitchen, breakfast bay, and family room with a fireplace are all open to one another for a comfortable, casual atmosphere. The first-floor master suite indulges with numerous closets, a dressing room, and a fabulous bath. Upstairs, four more bedrooms are topped by tray ceilings—three have walk-in closets and two have private baths. The three-car garage boasts additional storage and a bonus room above.

REAR EXTERIOR

PLAN HPK2400037

SQUARE FOOTAGE: 5,169
BONUS SPACE: 565 SQ. FT.
BEDROOMS: 3
BATHROOMS: 4½
WIDTH: 98' - 5"
DEPTH: 126' - 11"
FOUNDATION: SLAB

ORDER ONLINE @ EPLANS.COM

Stunning with texture, style, and grace, this Floridian home amazes at first sight. The entry is bordered by twin carousel bays and opens to an elegant floor plan. Intricate ceiling treatments in the dining room and study lend an extra touch of glamour. The living room is ahead, complete with a fireplace and sliding glass walls that allow the outdoors in. The right wing is entirely devoted to the master suite, presenting a sunny sitting area, French doors to the lanai, and views of the master garden out of the exquisite bath. On the left side of the plan, light streams into the gourmet kitchen from the family room and breakfast nook. A courtyard at the rear features a fireplace and outdoor kitchen.

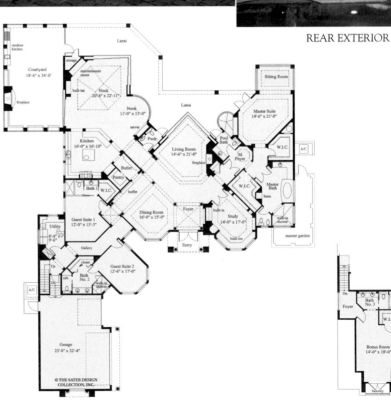

PLAN HPK2400038

FIRST FLOOR: 4,784 SQ. FT.
SECOND FLOOR: 481 SQ. FT.
TOTAL: 5,265 SQ. FT.
BEDROOMS: 4
BATHROOMS: 6½
WIDTH: 106' - 6"
DEPTH: 106' - 0"
FOUNDATION: Slab

ORDER ONLINE @ EPLANS.COM

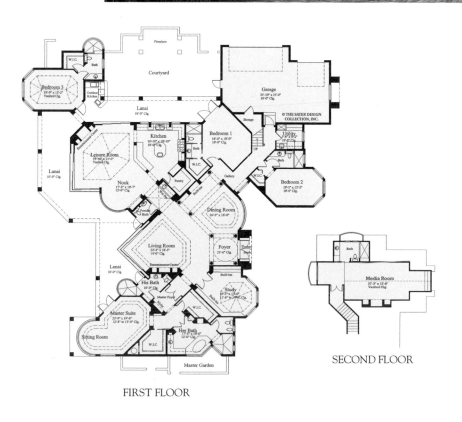

FIRST FLOOR

SECOND FLOOR

Dual bay windows create a sense of symmetry on the front of this magnificent Floridian design. Natural light is abundant throughout the interior, with window walls and sliding glass doors in virtually every room. Entertaining is a snap in the elegant dining room and angled living room. A diamond-shaped leisure room is the perfect family gathering spot, and an oversized kitchen makes whipping up gourmet meals a breeze. Bedrooms are separated to ensure privacy and quiet for family and guests. The master suite is a compelling hideaway with a bowed sitting area, His and Hers baths, and convenient proximity to the refined study. A media room on the upper level provides a great place to settle in with your favorite movie.

PLAN HPK2400039

MAIN LEVEL: 2,959 SQ. FT.
UPPER LEVEL: 1,055 SQ. FT.
LOWER LEVEL: 1,270 SQ. FT.
TOTAL: 5,284 SQ. FT.
BEDROOMS: 4
BATHROOMS: 5½
WIDTH: 110' - 4"
DEPTH: 72' - 5"
FOUNDATION: SLAB, FINISHED
WALKOUT BASEMENT

ORDER ONLINE @ EPLANS.COM

UPPER LEVEL

MAIN LEVEL

LOWER LEVEL

Designed for a sloping lot, this fantastic Mediterranean home features all the views to the rear, making it the perfect home for an ocean, lake, or golf-course view. Inside, the great room features a rear wall of windows. The breakfast room, kitchen, dining room, and master suite also feature rear views. A three-level series of porches is located on the back for outdoor relaxing. Two bedroom suites are found upstairs, each with a private bath and a porch. The basement of this home features another bedroom suite and a large game room. An expandable area can be used as an office or Bedroom 5.

PLAN HPK2400040

FIRST FLOOR: 4,666 SQ. FT.
SECOND FLOOR: 626 SQ. FT.
TOTAL: 5,292 SQ. FT.
BEDROOMS: 4
BATHROOMS: 5½
WIDTH: 100' - 8"
DEPTH: 134' - 5"
FOUNDATION: SLAB

ORDER ONLINE @ EPLANS.COM

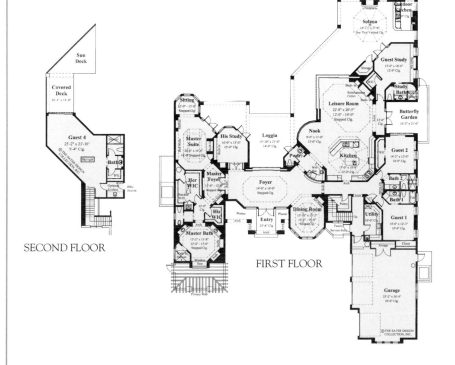

SECOND FLOOR

FIRST FLOOR

A tall entry and broad footprint give this European home a commanding presence. Upon entering, a large foyer gives way to a loggia beyond, the master wing on the left, and the remaining rooms to the right. The master bedroom's built-ins provide a place to display treasures and a sitting room for relaxing while surrounded by slender windows with backyard views. His and Hers closets flank the hallway leading to the master bath with a corner tub, dual vanity sinks, and a built-in window seat. The right wing of the home opens with a formal dining room on the right and a kitchen entrance past the wet bar on the left. The open island kitchen overlooks the breakfast and leisure rooms. Across the hall, a butterfly garden brings nature indoors and a guest study provides a private space off the solana and outdoor kitchen. Three guest suites—one upstairs, two down—provide excellent quarters for visitors.

PLAN HPK2400041

FIRST FLOOR: 4,431 SQ. FT.
SECOND FLOOR: 989 SQ. FT.
TOTAL: 5,420 SQ. FT.
BEDROOMS: 5
BATHROOMS: 5½
WIDTH: 105' - 7"
DEPTH: 100' - 4"
FOUNDATION: SLAB

ORDER ONLINE @ EPLANS.COM

REAR EXTERIOR

SECOND FLOOR

Sprawling space, wide open rooms, and a flowing indoor/outdoor relationship are Mediterranean influences brought to life in this design. The covered rear porch includes a fireplace on one end and an outdoor kitchen at the other. The home is filled with appealing atmosphere, varying throughout with a variety of ceiling treatments. A split-bedroom design works wonders here as the master suite and to-die-for master bath encompass the entire left wing, leaving the right side to two family bedrooms with private baths and a game room. Another bed and bath, the home theater, and a meditation room reside on the second level. Enough storage for out-of-season decorations and clothing is also available.

FIRST FLOOR

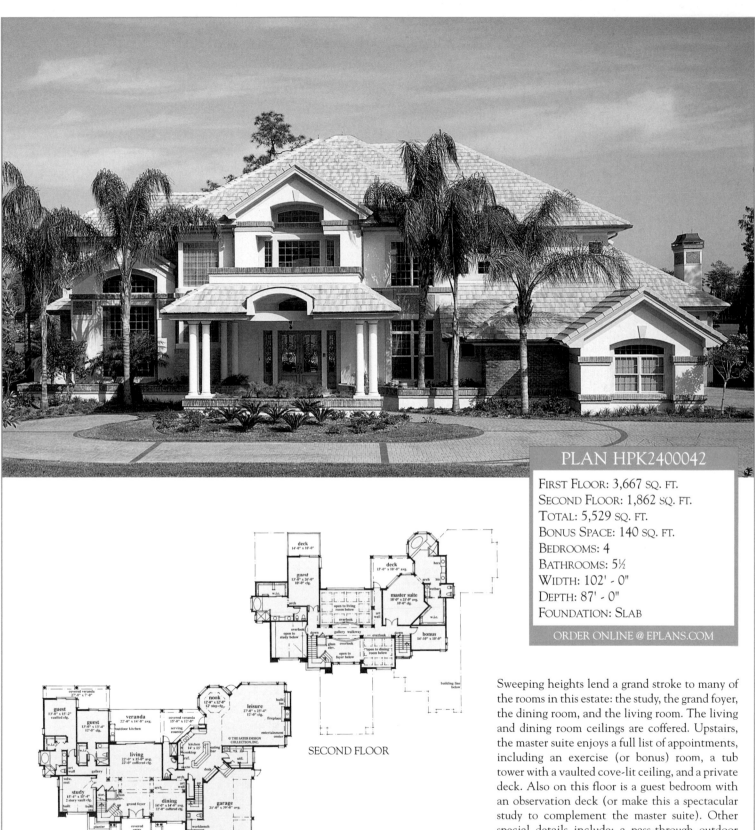

FIRST FLOOR

SECOND FLOOR

PLAN HPK2400042

FIRST FLOOR: 3,667 SQ. FT.
SECOND FLOOR: 1,862 SQ. FT.
TOTAL: 5,529 SQ. FT.
BONUS SPACE: 140 SQ. FT.
BEDROOMS: 4
BATHROOMS: 5½
WIDTH: 102' - 0"
DEPTH: 87' - 0"
FOUNDATION: SLAB

ORDER ONLINE @ EPLANS.COM

Sweeping heights lend a grand stroke to many of the rooms in this estate: the study, the grand foyer, the dining room, and the living room. The living and dining room ceilings are coffered. Upstairs, the master suite enjoys a full list of appointments, including an exercise (or bonus) room, a tub tower with a vaulted cove-lit ceiling, and a private deck. Also on this floor is a guest bedroom with an observation deck (or make this a spectacular study to complement the master suite). Other special details include: a pass-through outdoor bar, an outdoor kitchen, a workshop area, two verandas, and a glass elevator.

HELPFUL HINT! All plans in this magazine were drawn by designers working under strict industry standards.

PLAN HPK2400043

FIRST FLOOR: 4,208 SQ. FT.
SECOND FLOOR: 1,352 SQ. FT.
TOTAL: 5,560 SQ. FT.
BEDROOMS: 4
BATHROOMS: 4½ + ½
WIDTH: 94' - 0"
DEPTH: 68' - 0"
FOUNDATION: CRAWLSPACE, SLAB

ORDER ONLINE @ EPLANS.COM

Two-story pilasters create a sense of the Old South on the facade of this modern home, updating the classic Adam style. The foyer opens through an archway, announcing the breathtaking circular staircase. The formal dining room is situated on the right, and the private library is found to the left. The grand family room is crowned with a sloped ceiling. The angled, galley kitchen adjoins the breakfast nook; the butler's pantry facilitates service to the dining room. The master suite finds privacy on the left with an elegant sitting area defined with pillars. Two bedroom suites, each with walk-in closets, share the second floor with the game room.

REAR EXTERIOR

SECOND FLOOR

FIRST FLOOR

REAR EXTERIOR

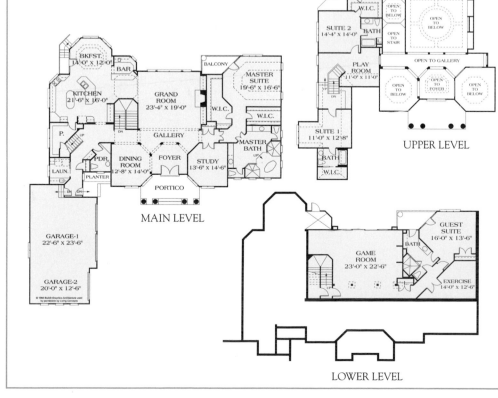

MAIN LEVEL

UPPER LEVEL

LOWER LEVEL

PLAN HPK2400044

MAIN LEVEL: 3,187 SQ. FT.
UPPER LEVEL: 1,000 SQ. FT.
LOWER LEVEL: 1,500 SQ. FT.
TOTAL: 5,687 SQ. FT.
BEDROOMS: 4
BATHROOMS: 4½
WIDTH: 85' - 4"
DEPTH: 90' - 10"
FOUNDATION: Finished Walkout
Basement

ORDER ONLINE @ EPLANS.COM

Situated below the gorgeous roof with a covered front porch supported by stately pillars, this Mediterranean beauty is three levels of luxury. A guest suite with full bath occupies the lower level, a prime location to take advantage of the exercise and game rooms. The main level is masterfully laid out: an extraordinary kitchen, breakfast room, and wet bar are to the far left; the master suite and bath are nestled to the far right; and the center of the home offers the grand room, dining room, and study for your enjoyment. Upstairs are the kids' play room, bedrooms and baths, along with amazing views of the two-story rooms below.

REAR EXTERIOR

SECOND FLOOR

FIRST FLOOR

PLAN HPK2400045

First Floor: 4,385 sq. ft.
Second Floor: 1,431 sq. ft.
Total: 5,816 sq. ft.
Bedrooms: 5
Bathrooms: 6
Width: 88' - 0"
Depth: 110' - 1"
Foundation: Slab

ORDER ONLINE @ EPLANS.COM

Low rooflines and grand arches lend a Mediterranean flavor to this contemporary estate. Lovely glass-paneled doors lead to an open interior defined by decorative columns, stone arches, and solid coffered ceilings. A formal living room boasts a fireplace, access to the veranda, and oversized windows for amazing views. Leisure space near the kitchen invites casual gatherings and allows the family to relax in front of a built-in entertainment center. A favorite feature, the outdoor kitchen encourages dining alfresco. A secluded master suite—with a sitting area, splendid bath, and access to the veranda—stretches across the left wing, which includes a quiet study with a vintage high-beamed ceiling. Among the four additional bedroom suites, one boasts a morning kitchen; two have access to a private deck or veranda.

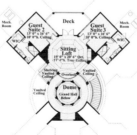

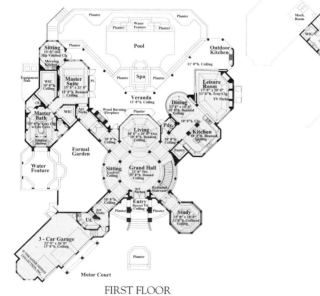

REAR EXTERIOR

PLAN HPK2400046

FIRST FLOOR: 4,715 SQ. FT.
SECOND FLOOR: 1,209 SQ. FT.
TOTAL: 5,924 SQ. FT.
BEDROOMS: 3
BATHROOMS: 3½
WIDTH: 117' - 7"
DEPTH: 131' - 2"
FOUNDATION: SLAB

ORDER ONLINE @ EPLANS.COM

FIRST FLOOR

SECOND FLOOR

Asymmetrical rooflines and stunning stucco walls announce an unrestrained interior that encourages "the good life." The entry opens to the grand hall—an open, light-filled retreat defined by massive columns and wide views. The heart of the plan is a living room set off by spectacular views of the veranda and luxurious pool area. The gourmet kitchen overlooks the formal dining room and the vaulted leisure room. The secluded master wing provides a separate sitting room with its own morning kitchen and access to a private area of the veranda. A rambling master bath surrounds a step-up whirlpool tub and offers a garden view. Upstairs, a spacious sitting loft leads outdoors to a wide deck. Each of two spacious guest suites provides a walk-in closet and luxury bath.

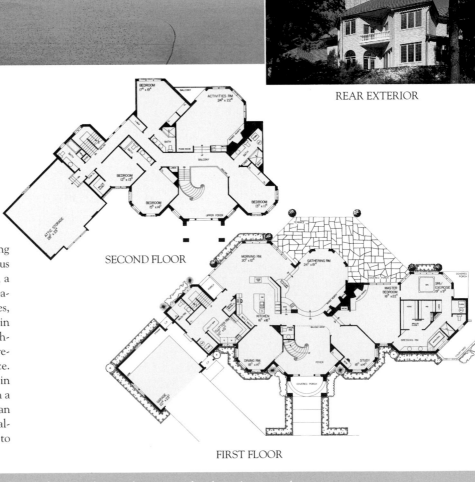

PLAN HPK2400047

FIRST FLOOR: 3,736 SQ. FT.
SECOND FLOOR: 2,264 SQ. FT.
TOTAL: 6,000 SQ. FT.
BEDROOMS: 5
BATHROOMS: 5½ + ½
WIDTH: 133' - 4"
DEPTH: 65' - 5"
FOUNDATION: SLAB

ORDER ONLINE @ EPLANS.COM

REAR EXTERIOR

SECOND FLOOR

FIRST FLOOR

The distinctive covered entry to this stunning manor, flanked by twin turrets, leads to a gracious foyer. The foyer opens to a formal dining room, a study, and a step-down gathering room. The spacious kitchen includes numerous amenities, including an island work station and a built-in desk. The adjacent morning room and the gathering room, with a wet bar and a raised-hearth fireplace, are bathed in light and open to the terrace. The secluded master suite offers two walk-in closets, a dressing area, and an exercise area with a spa. The second floor features four bedrooms and an oversized activities room with a fireplace and a balcony. Unfinished attic space can be completed to your specifications.

HELPFUL HINT!   A predrawn house plan is $8,000–$20,000 cheaper than a typical architect's custom design.

REAR EXTERIOR

SECOND FLOOR

FIRST FLOOR

PLAN HPK2400048

FIRST FLOOR: 5,265 SQ. FT.
SECOND FLOOR: 746 SQ. FT.
TOTAL: 6,011 SQ. FT.
BEDROOMS: 4
BATHROOMS: 4½
WIDTH: 100' - 0"
DEPTH: 140' - 0"
FOUNDATION: Slab

ORDER ONLINE @ EPLANS.COM

Passing the courtyard and beautifully arched entry, visitors will marvel at the intersecting foyer, which leads ahead to the living room and connects the left and right wings of the plan. The dining room and study flank the entryway, establishing the home's formal spaces. Ahead, the living room features one of the home's several fireplaces and a row of accent windows placed just below the astonishing 22-foot ceiling. A dramatic array of windows frames the amazing view of the plan's garden lanai and pool. Two bedrooms at the left of the plan are attended by full baths and walk-in closets. But the star of the show is the resplendent master suite, which incorporates all the luxury amenities appropriate to a home of this magnitude.

REAR EXTERIOR

PLAN HPK2400049

FIRST FLOOR: 4,742 SQ. FT.
SECOND FLOOR: 1,531 SQ. FT.
TOTAL: 6,273 SQ. FT.
BEDROOMS: 4
BATHROOMS: 4½ + ½
WIDTH: 96' - 0"
DEPTH: 134' - 8"
FOUNDATION: Slab

ORDER ONLINE @ EPLANS.COM

SECOND FLOOR

FIRST FLOOR

The majestic entrance is just the beginning of this magnificent estate. A short hallway to the right of the foyer leads into the master suite that comprises the entire right side of the plan downstairs. The master bath offers dual vanities, a large shower, and a tub with an enclosed view of a privacy garden. His and Hers walk-in closets lead from the dressing area, which flows easily into the bedroom. Within the bedroom, a sitting room offers a quiet retreat. The left side of the plan belongs to a spacious gourmet kitchen with an island snack bar, plenty of counter space, a breakfast nook, and a large leisure area. Adjacent to the kitchen is a guest bedroom with a private full bath. Upstairs there are two additional bedrooms, each with a full bath and walk-in closet, one with a balcony. A media room is the finishing touch on this masterpiece.

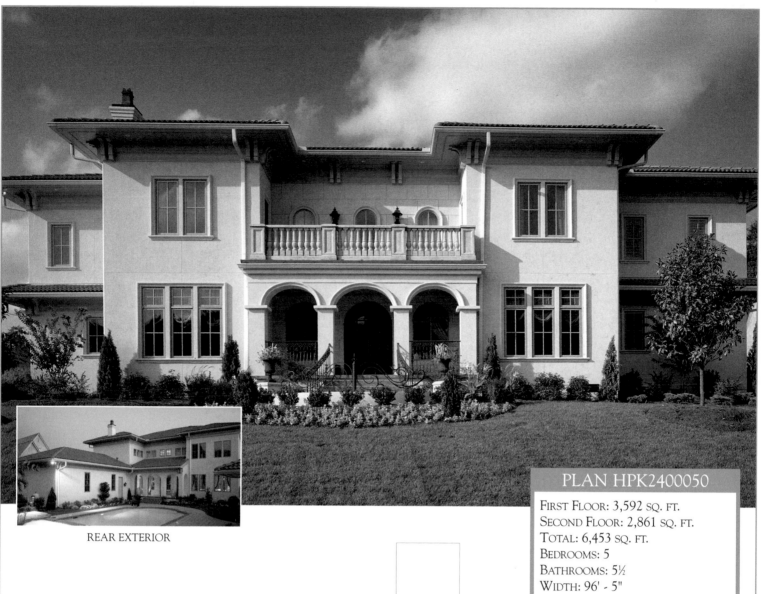

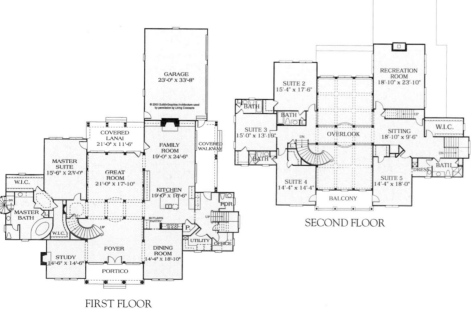

REAR EXTERIOR

PLAN HPK2400050

FIRST FLOOR: 3,592 SQ. FT.
SECOND FLOOR: 2,861 SQ. FT.
TOTAL: 6,453 SQ. FT.
BEDROOMS: 5
BATHROOMS: 5½
WIDTH: 96' - 5"
DEPTH: 91' - 6"
FOUNDATION: CRAWLSPACE

ORDER ONLINE @ EPLANS.COM

Stunning Mediterranean style gives this home a sense of palatial elegance. Arches frame the portico, which leads inside to an impressive two-story foyer. A study warmed by a fireplace is to the left and a formal dining room is introduced on the right. The first-floor master suite enjoys a deluxe whirlpool bath and two walk-in closets. The island kitchen opens to the casual family room, warmed by a second fireplace. Four additional suites reside upstairs for other family members. A romantic overlook views the great room and foyer. A sitting room is placed just outside of the second-floor recreation room.

FIRST FLOOR

SECOND FLOOR

REAR EXTERIOR

PLAN HPK2400051

First Floor: 3,874 sq. ft.
Second Floor: 2,588 sq. ft.
Total: 6,462 sq. ft.
Bedrooms: 4
Bathrooms: 5½ + ½
Width: 146' - 8"
Depth: 84' - 4"
Foundation: Slab

ORDER ONLINE @ EPLANS.COM

An oversized front entry beckons your attention to the wonderful amenities inside this home: a raised marble vestibule with a circular stair; a formal library and dining hall with views to the veranda and pool beyond; and a family gathering hall, open to the kitchen and connected to the outdoor grill. The master suite is embellished with a nature garden, His and Hers wardrobes, a fireplace, and an elegant bath. The second floor offers more living space with a media presentation room and a game room. Each of the family bedrooms features a private bath—reach one suite via a bridge over the porte cochere.

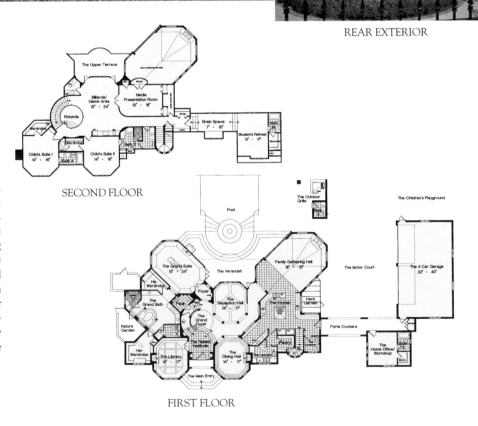

SECOND FLOOR

FIRST FLOOR

© Larry E. Belk Designs

PLAN HPK2400052

FIRST FLOOR: 5,394 SQ. FT.
SECOND FLOOR: 1,305 SQ. FT.
TOTAL: 6,699 SQ. FT.
BONUS SPACE: 414 SQ. FT.
BEDROOMS: 5
BATHROOMS: 3½ + ½
WIDTH: 124' - 10"
DEPTH: 83' - 2"
FOUNDATION: Crawlspace

ORDER ONLINE @ EPLANS.COM

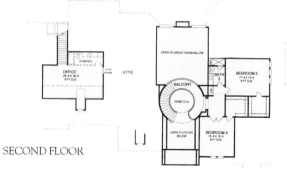

SECOND FLOOR

FIRST FLOOR

This elegant French Country estate features a plush world of luxury within. A beautiful curved staircase cascades into the welcoming foyer that is flanked by a formal living room and the dining room with a fireplace. A butler's pantry leads to the island kitchen, which is efficiently enhanced by a walk-in storage pantry. The kitchen easily serves the breakfast room. The covered rear porch is accessed from the media/family room and the great room warmed by a fireplace. The master suite is a sumptuous retreat highlighted by its lavish bath and two huge walk-in closets. Next door, double doors open to a large study. All family bedrooms feature walk-in closets. Bedrooms 2 and 3 share a bath. Upstairs, Bedrooms 4 and 5 share another hall bath. A home office is located above the three-car garage.

HELPFUL HINT! Bonus rooms generally are not calculated in the total square footage of a home.

PLAN HPK2400053

First Floor: 5,060 sq. ft.
Second Floor: 1,720 sq. ft.
Total: 6,780 sq. ft.
Bedrooms: 5
Bathrooms: 6
Width: 103' - 0"
Depth: 126' - 2"
Foundation: Slab

ORDER ONLINE @ EPLANS.COM

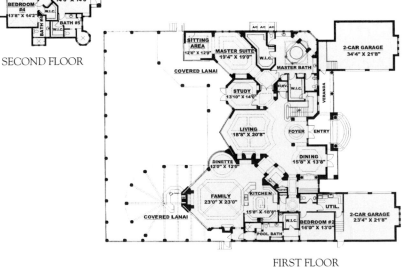

REAR EXTERIOR

SECOND FLOOR

FIRST FLOOR

This award-winning two-story home embraces many unique features. Entering through the stylish front steps and double entry doors provides a magnificent view of the pool area beyond the living room. A fireplace and built-in shelves grace one wall of the living room. The oversized family room features a built-in entertainment center and a second fireplace. The spacious master suite includes a large sitting area. The luxurious master bath features an oversized tub and a large dual-head shower area. Two huge walk-in closets and His and Hers water closets complete this bathroom design. The study with built-in bookshelves, large guest bedroom suite, powder room, pool bath, utility room, and two separate two-car garages complete the first floor. Large pocket sliders open to the covered lanai and outdoor kitchen area.

REAR EXTERIOR

PLAN HPK2400054

FIRST FLOOR: 4,511 SQ. FT.
SECOND FLOOR: 2,295 SQ. FT.
TOTAL: 6,806 SQ. FT.
BEDROOMS: 4
BATHROOMS: 2½ + ½
WIDTH: 90' - 2"
DEPTH: 104' - 5"
FOUNDATION: FINISHED BASEMENT

ORDER ONLINE @ EPLANS.COM

FIRST FLOOR

SECOND FLOOR

This European-inspired home showcases exterior architectural elements such as elliptical arches, a parapet, limestone trim, and a solid brick facade. Ceiling treatments on the interior range from a spectacular octagonal skylight in the foyer to a stunning celestial dome above the breakfast area to beamed ceilings in the great and hearth rooms. The master bedroom pampers the homeowner with a whirlpool tub, two-person shower, dual vanities, and a bayed sitting area overlooking the rear yard. The terrace and rear porch combine to create an amazing outdoor living space. The second floor houses three additional bedrooms, each with a private bath and walk-in closet. Entertaining in the basement becomes more fun with a bar, gas fireplace, media area, and billiards room. An exercise room makes it fun and easy for the homeowner to stay in shape.

PLAN HPK2400055

FIRST FLOOR: 2,347 SQ. FT.
SECOND FLOOR: 1,800 SQ. FT.
THIRD FLOOR: 1,182 SQ. FT.
BASEMENT: 1,688 SQ. FT.
TOTAL: 7,017 SQ. FT.
BEDROOMS: 4
BATHROOMS: 5½
WIDTH: 75' - 5"
DEPTH: 76' - 4"
FOUNDATION: Finished Walkout
Basement

ORDER ONLINE @ EPLANS.COM

A level for everyone! On the first floor, there's a study with a full bath, a formal dining room, a grand room with a fireplace, and a fabulous kitchen with an adjacent morning room. The second floor contains three suites—each with a walk-in closet— two full baths, a loft, and a reading nook. A lavish master suite on the third floor is full of amenities, including His and Hers walk-in closets, a huge private bath, and a balcony. In the basement, casual entertaining takes off with a large gathering room, a home theater, and a spacious game room.

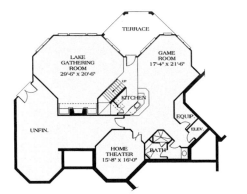

SECOND FLOOR

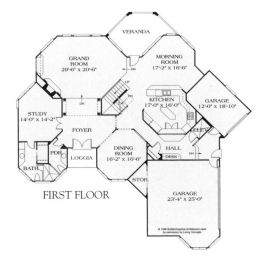

FIRST FLOOR

THIRD FLOOR

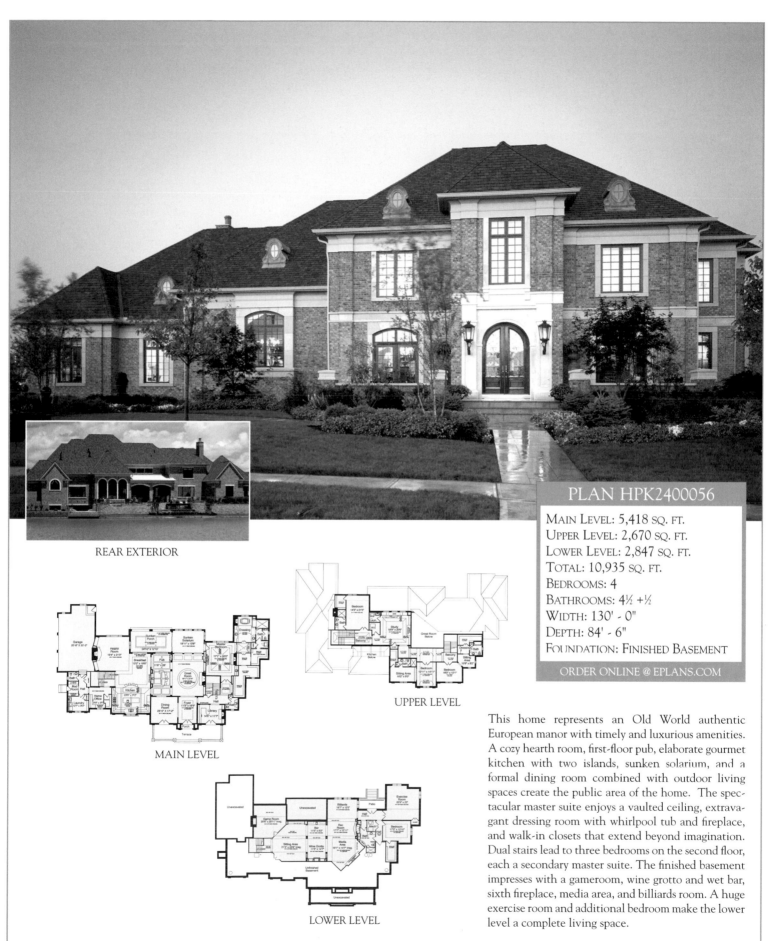

REAR EXTERIOR

MAIN LEVEL

UPPER LEVEL

LOWER LEVEL

PLAN HPK2400056

MAIN LEVEL: 5,418 SQ. FT.
UPPER LEVEL: 2,670 SQ. FT.
LOWER LEVEL: 2,847 SQ. FT.
TOTAL: 10,935 SQ. FT.
BEDROOMS: 4
BATHROOMS: 4½ +½
WIDTH: 130' - 0"
DEPTH: 84' - 6"
FOUNDATION: FINISHED BASEMENT

ORDER ONLINE @ EPLANS.COM

This home represents an Old World authentic European manor with timely and luxurious amenities. A cozy hearth room, first-floor pub, elaborate gourmet kitchen with two islands, sunken solarium, and a formal dining room combined with outdoor living spaces create the public area of the home. The spectacular master suite enjoys a vaulted ceiling, extravagant dressing room with whirlpool tub and fireplace, and walk-in closets that extend beyond imagination. Dual stairs lead to three bedrooms on the second floor, each a secondary master suite. The finished basement impresses with a gameroom, wine grotto and wet bar, sixth fireplace, media area, and billiards room. A huge exercise room and additional bedroom make the lower level a complete living space.

Laying It All Out

TRADITIONAL MATERIALS SURROUND A CONTEMPORARY INTERIOR DESIGN

ABOVE: A stone retaining wall and rock gardens present a welcome contrast to the softly curved and colorful landscape.

Curving, well-groomed landscaping and hardscaping complement a stone-and-siding exterior with multiple gables and a clerestory shed dormer. A robust footprint contributes to the home's contemporary residential design.

Inside, rooms are laid out in a popular order that promotes both style and functionality. The formal rooms—dining and living rooms—are at the front of the home, flanking the foyer. Straight ahead, a great room features a fireplace and built-ins that reach a height equal to the towering window cluster overlooking the rear property. Casual rooms are to the right, where the kitchen has room for an island and a peninsula snack bar overlooks the hearth room and breakfast nook. There is also access to the back deck for seasonal entertaining.

ABOVE: A faux finish on the walls and sheer draperies add to the elegance of the formal dining room.

LEFT: The kitchen and hearth room share a large-tiled floor that visually creates even more space in these large rooms. Cabinetry conceals both appliances and media equipment.

BELOW AND OPPOSITE: Long, straight curtains emphasize the towering height of the great room windows. The extended mantel above the fireplace is large enough to frame the massive wall art. Built-in shelves provide niches for art and collectibles. A fanlight and sidelights bring in light from around the double-door front entry while a shed dormer lights from above.

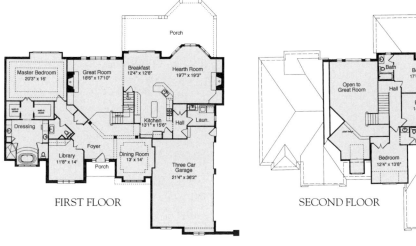

FIRST FLOOR

Master Bedroom 20'3" x 16'
Great Room 18'6" x 17'10"
Breakfast 12'4" x 12'8"
Hearth Room 19'7" x 19'3"
Dressing
Kitchen 13'1" x 15'6"
Laun.
Hall
Library 11'8" x 14'
Foyer
Dining Room 13' x 14'
Porch
Three Car Garage 21'4" x 36'2"
Porch

SECOND FLOOR

Bath
Bedroom 17'4" x 11'1"
Open to Great Room
Hall
Bedroom 14'8" x 11'3"
Bath
Bedroom 12'4" x 13'8"

PLAN HPK2400057

FIRST FLOOR: 2,702 SQ. FT.

SECOND FLOOR: 986 SQ. FT.

TOTAL: 3,688 SQ. FT.

BEDROOMS: 4

BATHROOMS: 3½

WIDTH: 75' - 0"

DEPTH: 64' - 11"

FOUNDATION: Unfinished
BASEMENT

ORDER ONLINE @ EPLANS.COM

ABOVE: Three windows with clean, modern lines light the master bath from just above a stepped garden tub.

In the left wing of the home, the first-floor master suite is secluded for privacy and contains two walk-in closets and a luxurious bath with a corner shower, garden tub, and two vanities.

Upstairs, two family bedrooms share a Jack-and-Jill bath, while a third bedroom has its own private full bath. A balcony hallway overlooks the great room below. ∎

REAR EXTERIOR

BONUS RM.
15-0 x 28-4

storage

attic storage

down

walk-in closet

railing

great room below

down

bath

attic storage

foyer below

walk-in closet

BED RM.
13-0 x 12-0

BED RM.
13-0 x 12-0

SECOND FLOOR

PATIO

STORAGE
10-4 x 6-4

BRKFST.
13-4 x 12-0

desk

pantry

PORCH

ovens

MASTER
BED RM.
16-0 x 17-0

fireplace

KITCHEN
13-4 x 12-8

GREAT RM.
20-0 x 16-0
(vaulted ceiling)

fireplace

shelves

walk-in closet

walk-in closet

GARAGE
22-0 x 31-0

balcony above

master bath

UTIL.
6-0 x 10-0

sto.

up

pd. rm.

lin.

© 2000 DAG
All rights reserved

DINING
13-0 x 12-0

FOYER
8-0 x 12-8

STUDY
13-0 x 12-0

PORCH

FIRST FLOOR

PLAN HPK2400058

FIRST FLOOR: 2,270 SQ. FT.
SECOND FLOOR: 685 SQ. FT.
TOTAL: 2,955 SQ. FT.
BONUS SPACE: 563 SQ. FT.
BEDROOMS: 3
BATHROOMS: 2½
WIDTH: 75' - 1"
DEPTH: 53' - 6"

ORDER ONLINE @ EPLANS.COM

Hipped rooflines, sunburst windows, and French-style shutters are the defining elements of this home's exterior. Inside, the foyer is flanked by the dining room and the study. Further on, the lavish great room can be entered by walking between two stately columns and is complete with a fireplace, built-in shelves, a vaulted ceiling, and views to the rear patio. The island kitchen easily accesses a pantry and a desk and flows into the bayed breakfast area. The first-floor master bedroom enjoys a fireplace, two walk-in closets, and an amenity-filled private bath. Two additional bedrooms reside upstairs, along with a sizable bonus room.

HELPFUL HINT!   Rest easy: All of our home designs conform to national uniform building codes.

© The Sater Design Collection, Inc.

PLAN HPK2400059

SQUARE FOOTAGE: 3,036
BEDROOMS: 4
BATHROOMS: 3½
WIDTH: 63' - 10"
DEPTH: 84' - 0"
FOUNDATION: SLAB

ORDER ONLINE @ EPLANS.COM

Here's a coastal cottage with acres of charm, starting with the covered entry and glass-paneled front door. An open interior and walls of glass allow wide views and plenty of natural light. The living room opens to a rear lanai that features decorative columns and a built-in grill. Informal entertaining will be a breeze with the leisure room, kitchen, and breakfast nook. A split sleeping arrangement places the master suite to the right of the plan, near the study. The left side of the plan includes two additional bedrooms and a guest suite.

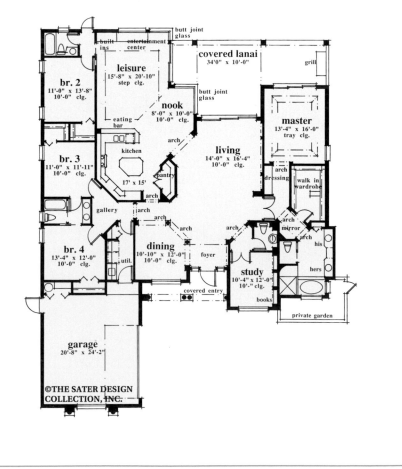

PLAN HPK2400060

FIRST FLOOR: 2,121 SQ. FT.
SECOND FLOOR: 920 SQ. FT.
TOTAL: 3,041 SQ. FT.
BEDROOMS: 4
BATHROOMS: 3
WIDTH: 63' - 0"
DEPTH: 63' - 0"
FOUNDATION: CRAWLSPACE, SLAB

ORDER ONLINE @ EPLANS.COM

SECOND FLOOR

FIRST FLOOR

A striking combination of brick and siding complements multipane windows and a columned entry to
create a fresh face on this classic design. The two-story
foyer opens to the formal living and dining rooms set
off by columned archways. Casual living space
includes a spacious family area open to the breakfast
room—bright with windows—and the kitchen. The
main-level master suite boasts two walk-in closets, an
angled whirlpool tub, a separate shower, and additional linen storage. A guest suite or family bedroom
with a full bath is positioned for privacy on the opposite side of the plan. Each of the two family bedrooms
on the upper level boasts a walk-in closet. The bedrooms share a full bath with separate dressing areas
and are open to a gallery hall that leads to a sizable
game room with attic access.

PLAN HPK2400061

First Floor: 1,415 sq. ft.
Second Floor: 1,632 sq. ft.
Total: 3,047 sq. ft.
Bedrooms: 4
Bathrooms: 3½
Width: 56' - 0"
Depth: 47' - 6"
Foundation: Crawlspace,
Unfinished Walkout Basement

ORDER ONLINE @ EPLANS.COM

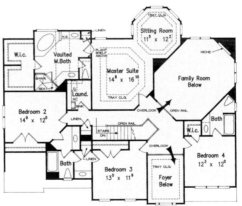

SECOND FLOOR

This impressive traditional design offers unique room placement to set it apart from other designs. The sun-drenched foyer leads to an angled two-story family room with a corner fireplace, a balcony overlook, and a pass-through to the island kitchen. The kitchen is a dream come true for any gourmand, with amenities that include a walk-in pantry, a writing desk, and plenty of counter space. The bayed breakfast nook, with its French-door access to the rear yard, will be a favorite place to congregate. A formal dining room and a living room with a private covered porch complete the first floor. Upstairs, two bedrooms share a full bath, and Bedroom 4 features its own bath and walk-in closet. The master bedroom suite offers a bayed sitting room—the perfect place to relax—and a master bath with a large walk-in closet.

FIRST FLOOR

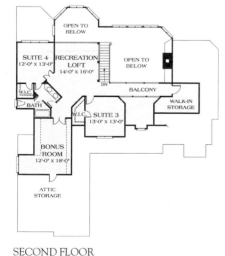

SECOND FLOOR

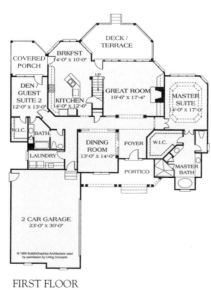

FIRST FLOOR

PLAN HPK2400062

FIRST FLOOR: 2,167 SQ. FT.
SECOND FLOOR: 891 SQ. FT.
TOTAL: 3,058 SQ. FT.
BONUS SPACE: 252 SQ. FT.
BEDROOMS: 4
BATHROOMS: 3
WIDTH: 64' - 10"
DEPTH: 74' - 0"
FOUNDATION: CRAWLSPACE

ORDER ONLINE @ EPLANS.COM

This traditional home contains elements of country style and a relaxed attitude that make it great for the waterfront or the suburbs. An inviting portico entry opens to the foyer, which leads ahead to the sun-drenched great room. A central staircase separates the great room from the gourmet kitchen that easily serves the dining room and sunny breakfast nook. A rear deck/terrace is accessible from this area. To the left, a den or guest suite has a semiprivate bath. The master suite claims the right wing, indulging in a magnificent bath and filled with natural light. Two bedrooms located upstairs share a full bath and access to a bonus room and recreation loft. A balcony over-look leads to convenient walk-in storage.

PLAN HPK2400063

First Floor: 2,035 sq. ft.
Second Floor: 1,028 sq. ft.
Total: 3,063 sq. ft.
Bedrooms: 4
Bathrooms: 3½
Width: 56' - 0"
Depth: 62' - 0"
Foundation: Unfinished Basement

ORDER ONLINE @ EPLANS.COM

This narrow-lot design would be ideal for a golf course or lakeside lot. Inside the arched entry, the formal dining room is separated from the foyer and the massive grand room by decorative pillars. At the end of the day, the family will enjoy gathering in the cozy keeping room with its fireplace and easy access to the large island kitchen and the sunny gazebo-style breakfast room. The master suite, located on the first floor for privacy, features a uniquely designed bedroom and a luxurious bath with His and Hers walk-in closets. Your family portraits and favorite art treasures can be displayed along the upstairs gallery, which shares space with three family bedrooms and two full baths.

SECOND FLOOR

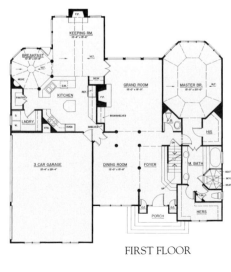

FIRST FLOOR

JOANNE E. LOFTUS

Helpful Hint! Reproducible plans are printed on vellum or Mylar.

82   Order blueprints anytime at 1-800-521-6797 or eplans.com

SECOND FLOOR

PLAN HPK2400064

FIRST FLOOR: 1,555 SQ. FT.
SECOND FLOOR: 1,523 SQ. FT.
TOTAL: 3,078 SQ. FT.
BEDROOMS: 5
BATHROOMS: 4
WIDTH: 54' - 0"
DEPTH: 44' - 8"
FOUNDATION: SLAB, UNFINISHED
WALKOUT BASEMENT

ORDER ONLINE @ EPLANS.COM

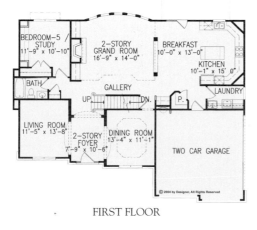

FIRST FLOOR

The main attraction of this home is found upstairs, in the form of an extravagant master suite. It features a tray ceiling, sitting area with bayed fireplace, angled bath with oversized tub, and a maze of a walk-in closet. As you emerge from the master suite, enjoy views of the grand room and foyer below. The fourth bedroom has a private bath, and bedroom #3 enjoys its own walk-in closet. You'll be certain to want to add the optional sunroom located off the breakfast nook. The foyer is flanked by a formal dining room, with tray ceiling, on the right, and a living room, through an elegant archway, to the left. The left-hand rear corner houses a study also suitable for a guest suite.

PLAN HPK2400065

FIRST FLOOR: 2,172 SQ. FT.
SECOND FLOOR: 962 SQ. FT.
TOTAL: 3,134 SQ. FT.
BEDROOMS: 4
BATHROOMS: 3
WIDTH: 50' - 0"
DEPTH: 67' - 6"

ORDER ONLINE @ EPLANS.COM

At home on just about any streetscape, this traditional home combines beautiful, low-maintenance siding with bold columns and multiple gables for added drama and appeal. A box-bay window frames the study/bedroom, while porches and a deck create outdoor living areas. French doors, windows, and an open floor plan allow this home to be airy and bright. Strategically placed columns help define rooms without enclosing space. A built-in desk provides a computer hub in a centralized location. With flexibility in mind, the upstairs can be tailored to a family's needs. A loft, which overlooks the great room, can be enclosed to form a bedroom. The bonus room can be a guest suite, home theater, or play room.

SECOND FLOOR

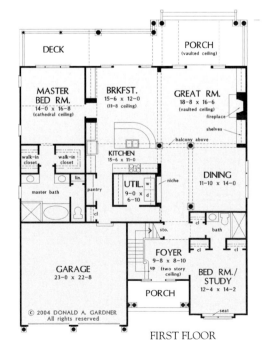

FIRST FLOOR

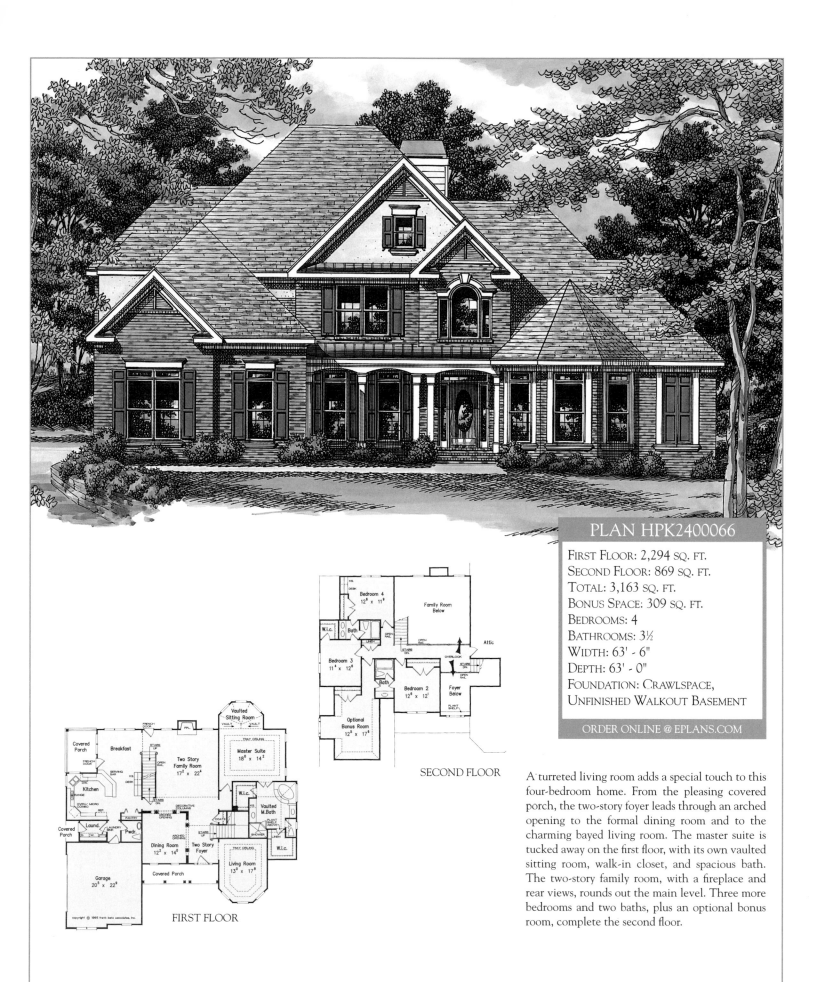

PLAN HPK2400066

FIRST FLOOR: 2,294 SQ. FT.
SECOND FLOOR: 869 SQ. FT.
TOTAL: 3,163 SQ. FT.
BONUS SPACE: 309 SQ. FT.
BEDROOMS: 4
BATHROOMS: 3½
WIDTH: 63' - 6"
DEPTH: 63' - 0"
FOUNDATION: CRAWLSPACE,
UNFINISHED WALKOUT BASEMENT

ORDER ONLINE @ EPLANS.COM

FIRST FLOOR

SECOND FLOOR

A turreted living room adds a special touch to this four-bedroom home. From the pleasing covered porch, the two-story foyer leads through an arched opening to the formal dining room and to the charming bayed living room. The master suite is tucked away on the first floor, with its own vaulted sitting room, walk-in closet, and spacious bath. The two-story family room, with a fireplace and rear views, rounds out the main level. Three more bedrooms and two baths, plus an optional bonus room, complete the second floor.

PLAN HPK2400067

FIRST FLOOR: 2,194 SQ. FT.
SECOND FLOOR: 971 SQ. FT.
TOTAL: 3,165 SQ. FT.
BONUS SPACE: 462 SQ. FT.
BEDROOMS: 5
BATHROOMS: 3½
WIDTH: 82' - 7"
DEPTH: 51' - 1"

ORDER ONLINE @ EPLANS.COM

Sophisticated and stately, this traditional home has an abundance of architectural interest and an open, family-efficient floor plan. Columns and an elegant balustrade create a regal entryway, joined by a box-bay window crowned with a metal roof and accentuated by a Palladian window. The foyer features a two-story cathedral ceiling and grand staircase. Interior columns and a balcony separate the great room with its fireplace, French doors, and built-in cabinetry. The kitchen is complete with a convenient central island and is open to the breakfast bay. The master bedroom includes a tray ceiling; two secondary bedrooms showcase vaulted ceilings.

SECOND FLOOR

FIRST FLOOR

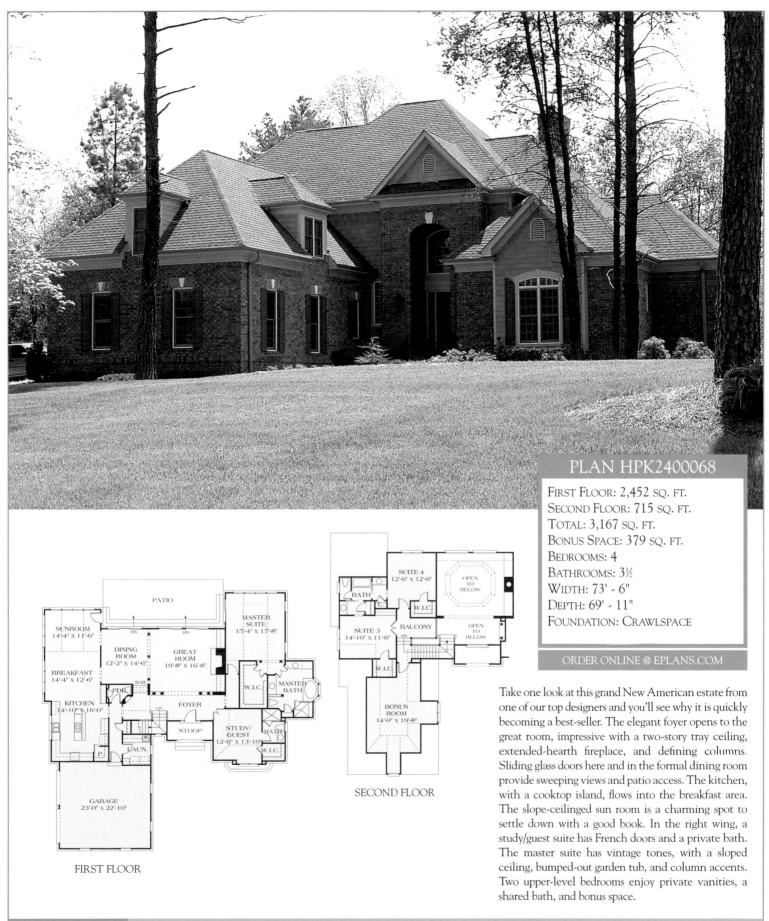

PLAN HPK2400068

First Floor: 2,452 sq. ft.

Second Floor: 715 sq. ft.

Total: 3,167 sq. ft.

Bonus Space: 379 sq. ft.

Bedrooms: 4

Bathrooms: 3½

Width: 73' - 6"

Depth: 69' - 11"

Foundation: Crawlspace

ORDER ONLINE @ EPLANS.COM

Take one look at this grand New American estate from one of our top designers and you'll see why it is quickly becoming a best-seller. The elegant foyer opens to the great room, impressive with a two-story tray ceiling, extended-hearth fireplace, and defining columns. Sliding glass doors here and in the formal dining room provide sweeping views and patio access. The kitchen, with a cooktop island, flows into the breakfast area. The slope-ceilinged sun room is a charming spot to settle down with a good book. In the right wing, a study/guest suite has French doors and a private bath. The master suite has vintage tones, with a sloped ceiling, bumped-out garden tub, and column accents. Two upper-level bedrooms enjoy private vanities, a shared bath, and bonus space.

FIRST FLOOR

SECOND FLOOR

Helpful Hint! A home automation upgrade provides all the wiring diagrams needed to build a Smart House.

PLAN HPK2400069

FIRST FLOOR: 2,153 SQ. FT.
SECOND FLOOR: 1,036 SQ. FT.
TOTAL: 3,189 SQ. FT.
BEDROOMS: 4
BATHROOMS: 3½
WIDTH: 72' - 0"
DEPTH: 60' - 6"
FOUNDATION: CRAWLSPACE,
UNFINISHED WALKOUT BASEMENT

ORDER ONLINE @ EPLANS.COM

A clever floor plan and stylish facade bring much-deserved accolades to this winsome design. Brick and vertical siding lend a fresh country look to the outside; inside, angles offer unique room arrangements to maximize space and flexibility. Upon entry, the two-story foyer opens on the left to a lovely columned dining room. The family room is ahead, with a soaring vaulted ceiling, warming fireplace, and a rear wall of windows. The bayed breakfast nook and vaulted keeping room offer endless views of the rear property. On the far right, the master suite hosts a vaulted bath with a step-up tub, His and Hers walk-in closets, and an optional sitting room that can also be used as a study. Upper-level bedrooms are designed for privacy, each with a distinctive amenity. A two-car garage, supplemented by an additional single garage, completes the plan.

SECOND FLOOR

FIRST FLOOR

PLAN HPK2400070

FIRST FLOOR: 2,198 SQ. FT.
SECOND FLOOR: 1,028 SQ. FT.
TOTAL: 3,226 SQ. FT.
BONUS SPACE: 466 SQ. FT.
BEDROOMS: 4
BATHROOMS: 3½
WIDTH: 72' - 8"
DEPTH: 56' - 6"
FOUNDATION: CRAWLSPACE

ORDER ONLINE @ EPLANS.COM

Designed for active lifestyles, this home caters to homeowners who enjoy dinner guests, privacy, luxurious surroundings, and open spaces. The foyer, parlor, and dining hall are defined by four sets of columns and share a gallery hall that runs through the center of the plan. The grand room opens to the deck/terrace, which is also accessed from the sitting area and morning room. The right wing of the plan contains the well-appointed kitchen. The left wing is dominated by the master suite with its sitting bay, fireplace, two walk-in closets, and compartmented bath.

PLAN HPK2400071

FIRST FLOOR: 2,450 SQ. FT.
SECOND FLOOR: 787 SQ. FT.
TOTAL: 3,237 SQ. FT.
BEDROOMS: 4
BATHROOMS: 3½
WIDTH: 68' - 11"
DEPTH: 65' - 7"
FOUNDATION: Unfinished
Basement

ORDER ONLINE @ EPLANS.COM

SECOND FLOOR

FIRST FLOOR

Striking gable rooflines and intriguing multipane windows of diverse shapes and sizes emphatically announce that this is an enchanting place to call "home." The mammoth country kitchen opens to a keeping room with a vault ceiling and fireplace and a cozy breakfast alcove with windows on five sides. The congenial formal dining room is easily served by the kitchen and opens conveniently to the dazzling and aptly named grand room. The front study, a quiet retreat, also enjoys a vault ceiling. An especially attractive feature of the first-floor master suite is a sitting room that opens to the rear yard. A bedroom with a private bath and sitting room shares the second level with two family bedrooms. Unfinished space on this floor can be used as you want. A three-car garage will ably protect the family's vehicles.

PLAN HPK2400072

FIRST FLOOR: 2,285 SQ. FT.
SECOND FLOOR: 956 SQ. FT.
TOTAL: 3,241 SQ. FT.
BONUS SPACE: 555 SQ. FT.
BEDROOMS: 5
BATHROOMS: 4
WIDTH: 57' - 3"
DEPTH: 65' - 5"

ORDER ONLINE @ EPLANS.COM

SECOND FLOOR

FIRST FLOOR

It's grand traditional homes like this one that bring character to the neighborhood. Brick and stone have a certain presence that evokes feelings of comfort, security, and, above all, home. Step inside the foyer and you'll find a smartly placed study or guest bedroom to the left and a columned, formal dining room to the right. Straight ahead is the hearth-warmed, two-story great room, ready for generations of family memories. The roomy island kitchen is conveniently adjacent to the great room, boasting miles of counter space and a sunny breakfast nook. The master suite takes up the entire right wing of the first floor, providing the homeowner with unparalleled luxury: two walk-in closets, a sitting room, and a bath that never ends await to pamper. Upstairs, three vaulted bedrooms share space with two baths, a huge bonus room, and a balcony overlook.

PLAN HPK2400073

FIRST FLOOR: 1,813 SQ. FT.
SECOND FLOOR: 1,441 SQ. FT.
TOTAL: 3,254 SQ. FT.
BEDROOMS: 5
BATHROOMS: 4
WIDTH: 49' - 0"
DEPTH: 59' - 0"
FOUNDATION: UNFINISHED
BASEMENT

ORDER ONLINE @ EPLANS.COM

Your future dream home awaits in this Early American Georgian design. Once inside, you are immediately enveloped by a sense of spaciousness. The open layout of the dining room and parlor follows the trend of informality in living areas. A guest room to the left enjoys a private entrance to a full bath. A fireplace in the living room warms the adjacent breakfast nook and island-cooktop kitchen. Upstairs, the master bedroom's intricate design, enhanced by tray ceilings, features a sitting area, a roomy bath, and a large walk-in closet with two entrances. Three additional family bedrooms and two full baths complete the second floor.

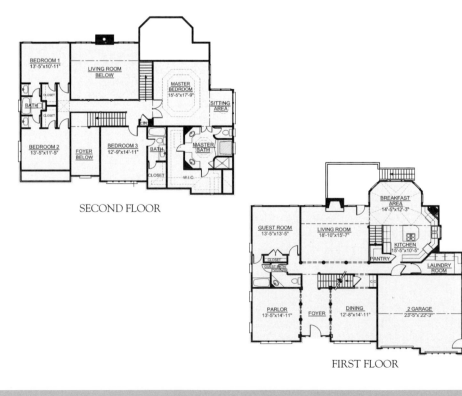

SECOND FLOOR

FIRST FLOOR

HELPFUL HINT!   A Smart House design enables universal control of home theater, security, and audio systems.

FIRST FLOOR

SECOND FLOOR

PLAN HPK2400074

FIRST FLOOR: 2,332 SQ. FT.
SECOND FLOOR: 942 SQ. FT.
TOTAL: 3,274 SQ. FT.
BONUS SPACE: 305 SQ. FT.
BEDROOMS: 4
BATHROOMS: 3½
WIDTH: 60' - 0"
DEPTH: 64' - 4"
FOUNDATION: CRAWLSPACE, SLAB,
UNFINISHED WALKOUT BASEMENT

ORDER ONLINE @ EPLANS.COM

A grand double-door entry welcomes all to this traditional home. Interesting ceiling treatments—
vaulted ceilings in the living areas and a tray
ceiling in the master suite—add a sense of style.
Other amenities in this suite include a bayed sitting
area, a luxurious private bath, and spacious His and
Hers walk-in closets. Fireplaces further enhance
the grand room and keeping room. The kitchen
features a large food-preparation island and is open
to a breakfast room. Upstairs, two additional bedrooms each have walk-in closets and share access
to a bathroom. Another bedroom, next to the
optional children's retreat, enjoys a private bath.

PLAN HPK2400075

First Floor: 2,136 sq. ft.

Second Floor: 1,201 sq. ft.

Total: 3,337 sq. ft.

Bonus Space: 482 sq. ft.

Bedrooms: 4

Bathrooms: 3½

Width: 62' - 0"

Depth: 78' - 10"

Foundation: Crawlspace

ORDER ONLINE @ EPLANS.COM

SECOND FLOOR

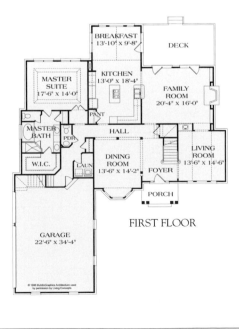

FIRST FLOOR

From formal entertaining in the elegant front rooms to relaxing on the back deck, this home is perfect for all aspects of your life. The generously sized kitchen offers a cooktop island, pantry, and plenty of counter and cabinet space. It is open to the breakfast area and family room, both of which open onto the wood deck. The family room is large enough for any family gathering and, with its high ceiling and cheerful fireplace, it will be well used. The master bedroom features a tray ceiling and a view of the back yard. Upstairs, the hallway leads to three bedrooms and a bonus room over the garage.

© The Sater Design Collection, Inc.

Magnificent brick and a Colonial-inspired facade make this home from one of our top designers a new favorite. Inside, the foyer opens to the living room/dining room combination, which allows flexibility in interior arrangement. The country kitchen serves the dining areas with ease and provides plenty of workspace for gourmet meal preparation. The leisure room entertains with a built-in media center and access to the rear veranda. Two family bedrooms share a full bath and extra hall storage. On the far left, the master suite is a dream, with a bayed window, oversized walk-in closets, and a grand spa bath with a whirlpool tub.

PLAN HPK2400077

FIRST FLOOR: 2,672 SQ. FT.

SECOND FLOOR: 687 SQ. FT.

TOTAL: 3,359 SQ. FT.

BONUS SPACE: 522 SQ. FT.

BEDROOMS: 4

BATHROOMS: 3

WIDTH: 72' - 6"

DEPTH: 64' - 5"

ORDER ONLINE @ EPLANS.COM

A brick exterior mixed with cedar shakes creates an intriguing facade for this four-bedroom custom home with a dramatic hipped roof and dual chimneys. This home features formal living and dining rooms as well as a more casual family room and breakfast area. The dining room is defined by well-placed interior columns. A second-floor balcony overlooks the vaulted living room, while the family room is expanded by a 13-foot ceiling. Two staircases make access to the second floor convenient from anywhere in the home. A bedroom/study and the master suite are located on the first floor, while the second floor features two more bedrooms and a bonus room.

SECOND FLOOR

FIRST FLOOR

© 2004 Donald A. Gardner, Inc.

SECOND FLOOR

PLAN HPK2400078

FIRST FLOOR: 2,562 SQ. FT.
SECOND FLOOR: 805 SQ. FT.
TOTAL: 3,367 SQ. FT.
BONUS SPACE: 622 SQ. FT.
BEDROOMS: 4
BATHROOMS: 4
WIDTH: 87' - 7"
DEPTH: 59' - 6"

ORDER ONLINE @ EPLANS.COM

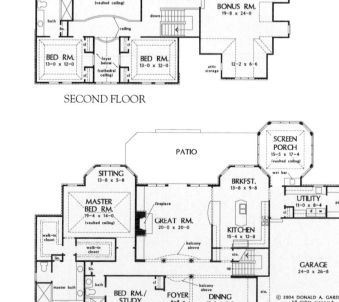

FIRST FLOOR

Evoking stately manors of the past, this traditional plan would be at home in any neighborhood. Inside, the design balances formal and informal spaces. Decorative windows usher in natural light, while columns and built-in cabinetry enhance elegance. A formal dining room and study flank the lofty foyer; beyond, the gallery gives way to a soaring great room. The common spaces offer all the latest amenities to enhance family life, such as a vast island kitchen, walk-in pantry, and a utility/mud room just inside the garage. A high-ceilinged screened porch will become a favorite place to enjoy the summer breezes. In a quiet corner of the first floor, the master suite offers all the necessary luxuries to help reduce the stress of everyday life. Children or guests will enjoy the privacy of the two upstairs bedrooms and baths, and the generous bonus space is large enough to accommodate several uses.

HELPFUL HINT!   Reproducible sets include a license to build the home once.

PLAN HPK2400079

First Floor: 2,174 sq. ft.

Second Floor: 1,241 sq. ft.

Total: 3,415 sq. ft.

Bonus Space: 347 sq. ft.

Bedrooms: 4

Bathrooms: 3½

Width: 61' - 4"

Depth: 68' - 8"

Foundation: Crawlspace

ORDER ONLINE @ EPLANS.COM

An impressive facade of stucco and stone and gabled peaks highlights the exterior of this plan. A loggia welcomes you inside to the foyer flanked by a study/library with a fireplace and the formal dining room brightened by a bay window. A gallery hall leads to other areas of the home, including a guest suite with a private bath, the grand room warmed by an impressive hearth, and the island kitchen overlooking the morning room. Upstairs, the master suite features a private fireplace, His and Hers walk-in closets, and a lavish bath. The second-floor game room is a spacious addition.

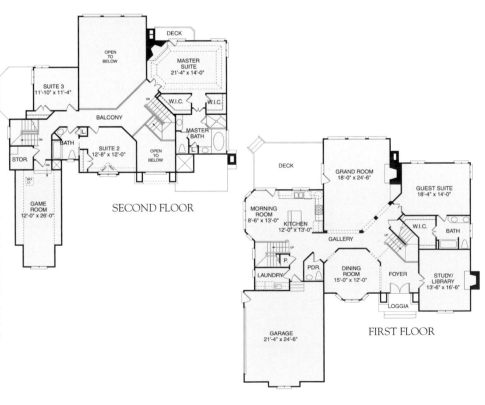

SECOND FLOOR

FIRST FLOOR

© Larry E. Belk Designs

© Larry E. Belk Designs

PLAN HPK2400080

SQUARE FOOTAGE: 3,426
BEDROOMS: 4
BATHROOMS: 2½
WIDTH: 78' - 6"
DEPTH: 82' - 4"
FOUNDATION: CRAWLSPACE, SLAB

ORDER ONLINE @ EPLANS.COM

One-story living takes off in this brick traditional home. Formal living areas flanking the entry are enhanced with 10-foot ceilings and open views to the great room. The great room features a 12-foot ceiling and is accented by a fireplace and expansive windows. The island kitchen has a sunny breakfast nook and easy passage to the dining room. A luxurious owners bedroom contains a spa-style bath with a raised corner whirlpool tub and a special exercise room. Three bedrooms share a full hall bath.

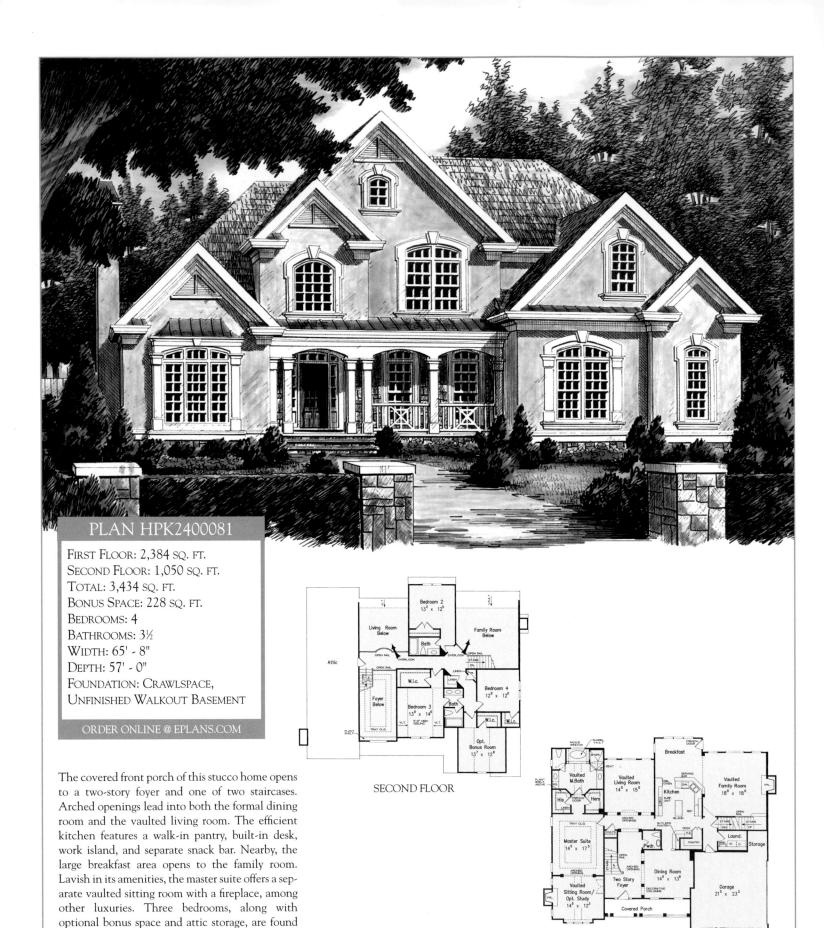

PLAN HPK2400081

FIRST FLOOR: 2,384 SQ. FT.
SECOND FLOOR: 1,050 SQ. FT.
TOTAL: 3,434 SQ. FT.
BONUS SPACE: 228 SQ. FT.
BEDROOMS: 4
BATHROOMS: 3½
WIDTH: 65' - 8"
DEPTH: 57' - 0"
FOUNDATION: CRAWLSPACE,
UNFINISHED WALKOUT BASEMENT

ORDER ONLINE @ EPLANS.COM

The covered front porch of this stucco home opens
to a two-story foyer and one of two staircases.
Arched openings lead into both the formal dining
room and the vaulted living room. The efficient
kitchen features a walk-in pantry, built-in desk,
work island, and separate snack bar. Nearby, the
large breakfast area opens to the family room.
Lavish in its amenities, the master suite offers a separate vaulted sitting room with a fireplace, among
other luxuries. Three bedrooms, along with
optional bonus space and attic storage, are found
on the second floor.

SECOND FLOOR

FIRST FLOOR

PLAN HPK2400082

FIRST FLOOR: 2,468 SQ. FT.
SECOND FLOOR: 981 SQ. FT.
TOTAL: 3,449 SQ. FT.
BEDROOMS: 4
BATHROOMS: 4
WIDTH: 58' - 7"
DEPTH: 79' - 6"

ORDER ONLINE @ EPLANS.COM

FIRST FLOOR

SECOND FLOOR

Pillars, arches, and banding lend a subtle sophistication to the brick exterior. A Palladian window tops a triple window, which is capped by a metal roof, while a patio and porches—including a screened one—extend living to the outdoors. Opening to the dining room and study/bedroom, the foyer leads to a gallery, which features an art niche. Columns, built-in cabinetry, and ceiling treatments enhance the open floor plan, while a butler's pantry, home office, and spacious laundry provide convenience. Upstairs, a generous loft separates the secondary bedrooms and provides enough room for a recreational area or second-floor study, and a versatile bonus room adds more flex space. The balcony visually connects both floors.

PLAN HPK2400083

FIRST FLOOR: 2,550 SQ. FT.
SECOND FLOOR: 917 SQ. FT.
TOTAL: 3,467 SQ. FT.
BONUS SPACE: 736 SQ. FT.
BEDROOMS: 4
BATHROOMS: 5
WIDTH: 61' - 6"
DEPTH: 85' - 0"
FOUNDATION: CRAWLSPACE, SLAB,
UNFINISHED WALKOUT BASEMENT

ORDER ONLINE @ EPLANS.COM

Fanciful touches like a swooping roofline and over-flowing window boxes lend a fairy-tale charm to this country-style home, while a courtyard entry and a thoughtful floorplan make it practical as well. The fantasy continues inside as luxury features turn up around every corner. Vaulted ceilings, multiple fire-places, built-in cabinetry, and French doors really do make this home a dream come true, while four spa-cious bedrooms and baths add to its functionality.

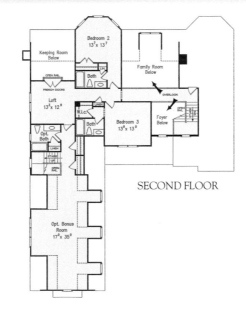

SECOND FLOOR

FIRST FLOOR

HELPFUL HINT!   Call one of our home plan experts about our customization services. Make your plan perfect.

102   ORDER BLUEPRINTS ANYTIME AT 1-800-521-6797 OR EPLANS.COM

PLAN HPK2400084

First Floor: 2,511 sq. ft.
Second Floor: 1,062 sq. ft.
Total: 3,573 sq. ft.
Bonus Space: 465 sq. ft.
Bedrooms: 4
Bathrooms: 3½
Width: 84' - 11"
Depth: 55' - 11"

ORDER ONLINE @ EPLANS.COM

SECOND FLOOR

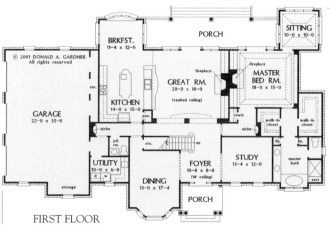

FIRST FLOOR

An abundance of windows and an attractive brick facade enhance the exterior of this traditional two-story home. Inside, a study and formal dining room flank the two-story foyer. Fireplaces warm both the great room and first-floor master suite. The suite also provides a separate sitting room, two walk-in closets, and a private bath. The island kitchen extends into the breakfast room. The second floor features three additional family bedrooms, two baths, and a bonus room fit for a home office.

PLAN HPK2400085

First Floor: 2,528 sq. ft.
Second Floor: 1,067 sq. ft.
Total: 3,595 sq. ft.
Bedrooms: 4
Bathrooms: 3½ + ½
Width: 69' - 2"
Depth: 73' - 10"
Foundation: Slab

ORDER ONLINE @ EPLANS.COM

Fine brick detailing and graceful gables enhance the elegance of this home. Upon entering, one steps into a two-story foyer showcasing a graceful curved staircase and the dining room. Situated with views to the side and rear of the home, the great room is designed with an offset perfect for a grand piano or game table. The kitchen and breakfast room are centrally located and open to the patio. The master suite features a sitting area and luxury bath, and the second floor's three bedrooms, two baths, and a game room complete the roomy accommodations.

SECOND FLOOR

FIRST FLOOR

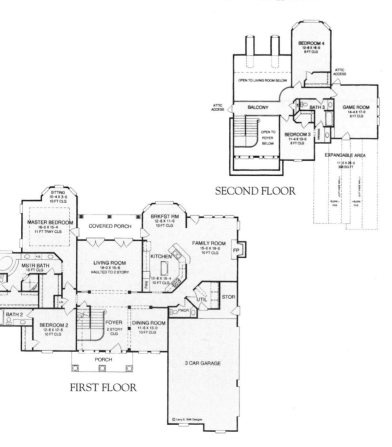

SECOND FLOOR

BEDROOM 4
12-6 X 16-0
8 FT CLG

ATTIC ACCESS

OPEN TO LIVING ROOM BELOW

ATTIC ACCESS

BALCONY

BATH 3

GAME ROOM
14-4 X 17-0
8 FT CLG

OPEN TO FOYER BELOW

BEDROOM 3
11-4 X 13-0
8 FT CLG

EXPANDABLE AREA
11-0 X 28-0
308 SQ FT

FIRST FLOOR

SITTING
10-4 X 3-6
10 FT CLG

MASTER BEDROOM
16-0 X 15-4
11 FT TRAY CLG

COVERED PORCH

BRKFST RM
12-6 X 11-0
10 FT CLG

MSTR BATH
10 FT CLG

LIVING ROOM
19-0 X 15-6
VAULTED TO 2 STORY

KITCHEN

FAMILY ROOM
15-0 X 19-0
10 FT CLG

FP

UTIL

STOR

BATH 2

BEDROOM 2
12-6 X 12-6
10 FT CLG

FOYER
2 STORY CLG

DINING ROOM
11-6 X 13-0
10 FT CLG

PWDR

PORCH

3 CAR GARAGE

© Larry E. Belk Designs

PLAN HPK2400086

FIRST FLOOR: 2,657 SQ. FT.
SECOND FLOOR: 1,026 SQ. FT.
TOTAL: 3,683 SQ. FT.
BONUS SPACE: 308 SQ. FT.
BEDROOMS: 4
BATHROOMS: 3½
WIDTH: 75' - 8"
DEPTH: 74' - 2"
FOUNDATION: CRAWLSPACE, SLAB,
UNFINISHED BASEMENT

ORDER ONLINE @ EPLANS.COM

This breathtaking Traditional manor looks great from the curb, but it is the interior that will steal your heart. The entry is lit by twin two-story Palladian windows for subtle drama. On the right, the dining room is defined by columns. The living room makes an elegant impression with a vaulted ceiling and French doors to the rear porch. The kitchen is nearby and sports a "boomerang" counter and a central island. A breakfast bay creates a cheerful place for casual meals. The family room is warmed by a fireplace and brightened by a rear wall of windows. The master suite is in the left wing, decadent with a bayed sitting area, porch access, and an indulgent spa bath. A nearby bedroom makes a great guest suite or home office. Upstairs, two lovely bedrooms share a full bath and a game room.

PLAN HPK2400087

FIRST FLOOR: 2,908 SQ. FT.
SECOND FLOOR: 790 SQ. FT.
TOTAL: 3,698 SQ. FT.
BONUS SPACE: 521 SQ. FT.
BEDROOMS: 4
BATHROOMS: 4½
WIDTH: 86' - 11"
DEPTH: 59' - 5"

ORDER ONLINE @ EPLANS.COM

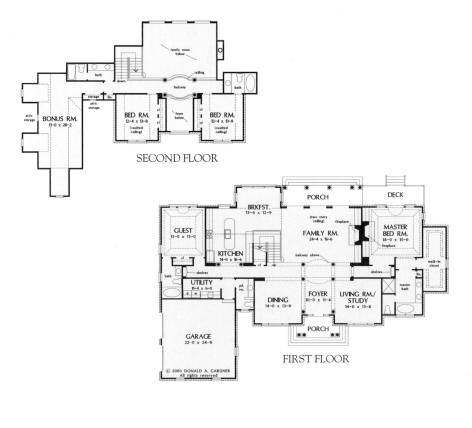

SECOND FLOOR

FIRST FLOOR

A stately hipped roof crowns this impressive executive home's brick exterior, which includes arch-topped windows, keystones and a covered entry with a balustrade. The spacious floor plan boasts formal and casual living areas. A two-story ceiling in the foyer and family room highlights an exciting curved balcony on the second floor. The generously proportioned kitchen includes a center island sink and plenty of work space. Distinctive shelving is built into either end of the home's center hall. The master suite and a guest suite, each with tray ceilings and private baths, are located on the first floor. Two vaulted bedrooms, two full baths and a bonus room can be found upstairs.

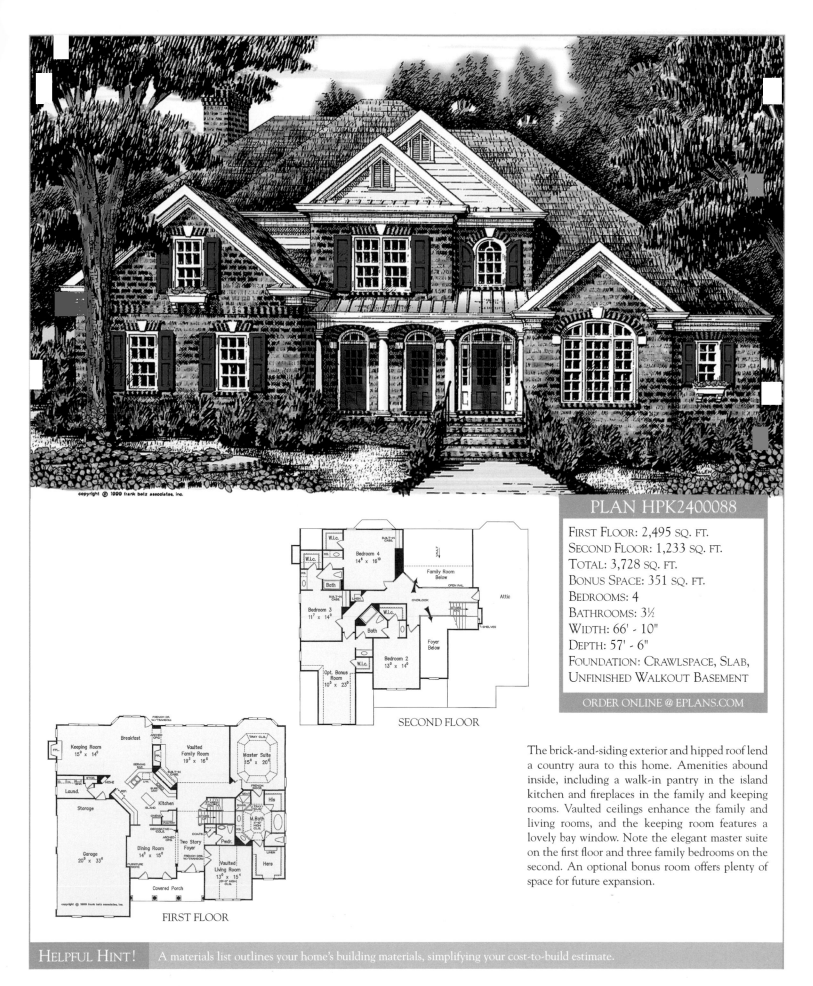

PLAN HPK2400088

FIRST FLOOR: 2,495 SQ. FT.
SECOND FLOOR: 1,233 SQ. FT.
TOTAL: 3,728 SQ. FT.
BONUS SPACE: 351 SQ. FT.
BEDROOMS: 4
BATHROOMS: 3½
WIDTH: 66' - 10"
DEPTH: 57' - 6"
FOUNDATION: CRAWLSPACE, SLAB,
UNFINISHED WALKOUT BASEMENT

ORDER ONLINE @ EPLANS.COM

SECOND FLOOR

FIRST FLOOR

The brick-and-siding exterior and hipped roof lend a country aura to this home. Amenities abound inside, including a walk-in pantry in the island kitchen and fireplaces in the family and keeping rooms. Vaulted ceilings enhance the family and living rooms, and the keeping room features a lovely bay window. Note the elegant master suite on the first floor and three family bedrooms on the second. An optional bonus room offers plenty of space for future expansion.

PLAN HPK2400089

First Floor: 2,665 sq. ft.
Second Floor: 1,081 sq. ft.
Total: 3,746 sq. ft.
Bedrooms: 4
Bathrooms: 3½
Width: 88' - 0"
Depth: 52' - 6"
Foundation: Unfinished
Walkout Basement

ORDER ONLINE @ EPLANS.COM

This New American home with country flourishes features a stately exterior appearance with brick, stone, and cedar siding and a large front porch. The great room and hearth room/breakfast area offer grand views to the rear yard, where a large deck complements outdoor activities. A spacious butler's pantry offers serving convenience and added storage for formal dining. A library with magnificent built-in shevles is located just off the foyer. A beamed ceiling and deluxe dressing area with a large walk-in closet and an oversized vanity pampers the homeowner with luxury. Fireplaces in the great room and hearth room add warmth and character to formal and informal gatherings. The work area of the kitchen features an oversized center island, while a bar with seating provides quick meals. Open stairs overlooking the great room lead to a spacious computer loft. Three additional bedrooms complete this home.

SECOND FLOOR

FIRST FLOOR

© Larry E. Belk Designs

PLAN HPK2400090

FIRST FLOOR: 2,319 SQ. FT.
SECOND FLOOR: 1,570 SQ. FT.
TOTAL: 3,889 SQ. FT.
BEDROOMS: 4
BATHROOMS: 3½
WIDTH: 72' - 0"
DEPTH: 58' - 0"
FOUNDATION: CRAWLSPACE

ORDER ONLINE @ EPLANS.COM

SECOND FLOOR

FIRST FLOOR

Fine brick detailing, multiple arches and gables, and a grand entry give this four-bedroom home plenty of charm. The graceful, window-filled entry leads to a foyer flanked by a formal dining room and a study perfect for a home office. The great room, directly ahead, offers a fireplace and access to outside. A butler's pantry is located between the kitchen and dining room. The master suite is on the first floor. On the second floor, three family bedrooms, each with a walk-in closet, share two baths and a game room.

PLAN HPK2400091

First Floor: 2,506 sq. ft.
Second Floor: 1,415 sq. ft.
Total: 3,921 sq. ft.
Bedrooms: 4
Bathrooms: 3½
Width: 80' - 5"
Depth: 50' - 4"
Foundation: Slab, Unfinished Basement

ORDER ONLINE @ EPLANS.COM

SECOND FLOOR

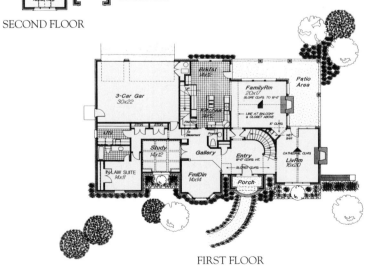

FIRST FLOOR

A stately two-story home with a gracious, manorly exterior features a large, arched entryway as its focal point. Excellent brick detailing and quoins help make this exterior one of a kind. The large, two-story family area is adjacent to the living room with its cathedral ceiling and formal fireplace—a convenient arrangement for entertaining large groups, or just a cozy evening at home. A wrapping patio area allows for dining outdoors. The large kitchen is centrally located, with a second stairway leading to the second floor. The master suite features a volume ceiling and a sitting area overlooking the rear yard. The huge master bath includes two walk-in closets. The upper balcony overlooks the family area and the entryway.

PLAN HPK2400092

First Floor: 2,751 sq. ft.
Second Floor: 1,185 sq. ft.
Total: 3,936 sq. ft.
Bedrooms: 4
Bathrooms: 3½
Width: 79' - 0"
Depth: 66' - 4"
Foundation: Slab, Unfinished Basement

ORDER ONLINE @ EPLANS.COM

SECOND FLOOR

FIRST FLOOR

With a grand brick facade, this home also boasts muntin windows, multilevel rooflines, cut-brick jack arches, and a beautifully arched entry. A cathedral-ceilinged living room, complete with a fireplace, and a family dining room flank the 20-foot-high entry. Relax in the family room, mix a drink from the wet bar, and look out through multiple windows to the covered veranda. A luxurious master suite includes a windowed sitting area looking over the rear view, private patio, full bath boasting a 10-foot ceiling, and a spacious walk-in closet On the second level, the three high-ceilinged bedrooms share two full baths and a study area with a built-in desk.

© The Sater Design Collection, Inc.

PLAN HPK2400093

FIRST FLOOR: 3,010 SQ. FT.
SECOND FLOOR: 948 SQ. FT.
TOTAL: 3,958 SQ. FT.
BEDROOMS: 4
BATHROOMS: 3½
WIDTH: 65' - 0"
DEPTH: 91' - 0"
FOUNDATION: Slab

ORDER ONLINE @ EPLANS.COM

This elegant home has all the angles covered, from its varied roofline to its interesting interior spaces. As you enter this unique design, a gracious living room opens up before you with views through dramatic corner windows to the covered lanai and beyond. A study with built-in bookcases and a formal dining room with a built-in server flank the front entrance. Built-in fixtures are also a feature of the large leisure area, kitchen, and adjacent breakfast nook. A breathtaking master suite enjoys its own private garden.

SECOND FLOOR

FIRST FLOOR

HELPFUL HINT! Eplans.com offers an Electrical Details set with residential electrical system information and diagrams.

112   ORDER blueprints anytime at 1-800-521-6797 or eplans.com

PLAN HPK2400094

FIRST FLOOR: 2,588 SQ. FT.
SECOND FLOOR: 1,375 SQ. FT.
TOTAL: 3,963 SQ. FT.
BONUS SPACE: 460 SQ. FT.
BEDROOMS: 4
BATHROOMS: 3½
WIDTH: 91' - 4"
DEPTH: 51' - 10"
FOUNDATION: CRAWLSPACE

ORDER ONLINE @ EPLANS.COM

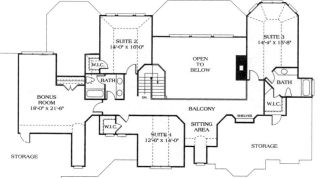

SECOND FLOOR

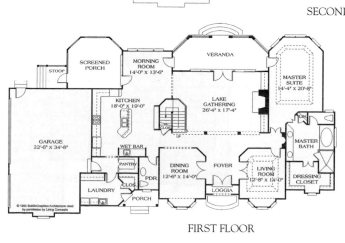

FIRST FLOOR

Although there are two entrances to this fine home, the one on the right is where friends and family should enter to truly absorb the grandeur of this design. The foyer is flanked by a bayed formal dining room and a bayed formal living room. Directly ahead is the lake gathering room, a spacious area with a welcoming fireplace and access to the rear veranda. The L-shaped kitchen, complete with an island, includes plenty of space and convenient features like a wet bar, walk-in pantry, and built-in shelves. Located on the first floor for privacy, the master suite is complete with a huge dressing closet, access to the veranda, and a lavish bath.

PLAN HPK2400097

FIRST FLOOR: 2,502 SQ. FT.
SECOND FLOOR: 1,645 SQ. FT.
TOTAL: 4,147 SQ. FT.
BEDROOMS: 5
BATHROOMS: 3½
WIDTH: 95' - 0"
DEPTH: 51' - 0"
FOUNDATION: UNFINISHED
BASEMENT

ORDER ONLINE @ EPLANS.COM

This Early American recreation is representative of the stately Federal styles of Colonial times. A beautifully curved stairway spirals into the foyer. To the left, double doors open to a family room. To the right, another set of double doors opens to a formal dining room. Straight ahead, the living room is brightened by a wall of windows overlooking the rear porch and is warmed by a cozy family fireplace. An island kitchen with a breakfast bar and a nook are located nearby. The garage conveniently connects directly to the kitchen. The first-floor master suite features rear-porch access, a private bath, and an enormous walk-in closet. Upstairs, four additional family bedrooms share two hall baths.

SECOND FLOOR

FIRST FLOOR

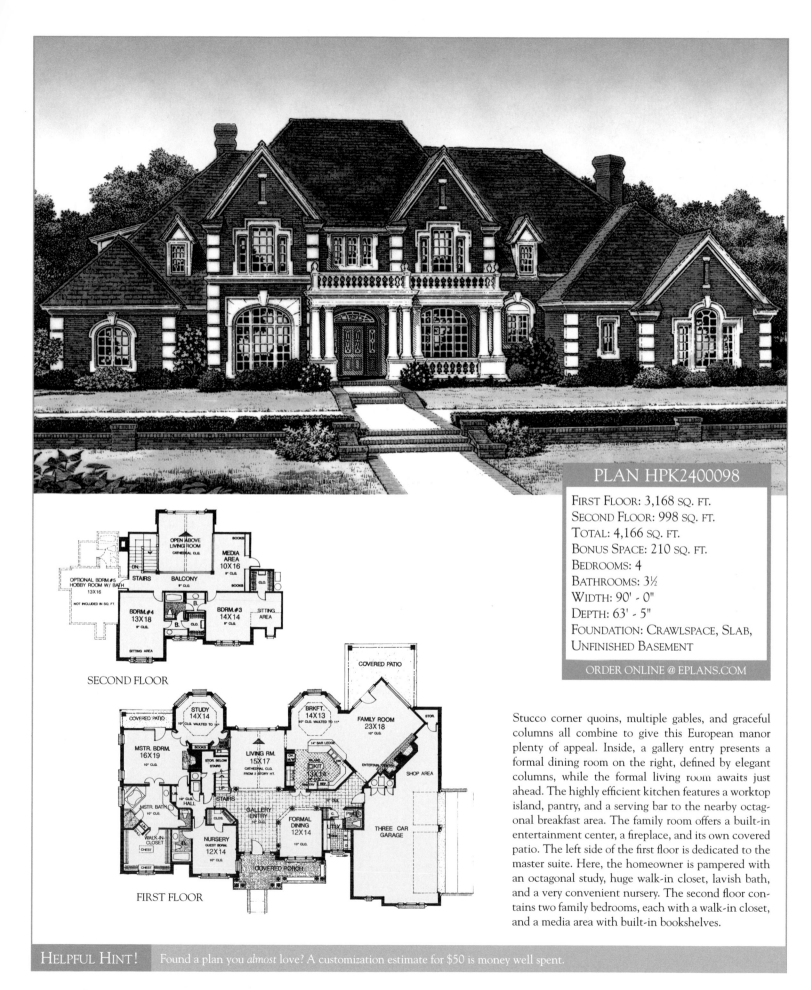

SECOND FLOOR

OPEN ABOVE LIVING ROOM
CATHEDRAL CLG.

MEDIA AREA
10X16
9' CLG.

BOOKS

STAIRS

BALCONY
9' CLG.

OPTIONAL BDRM.#5
HOBBY ROOM W/ BATH
13X16

NOT INCLUDED IN SQ. FT.

BDRM.#4
13X18
9' CLG.

BDRM.#3
14X14
9' CLG.

SITTING AREA

SITTING AREA

B.

B.

FIRST FLOOR

COVERED PATIO

STUDY
14X14
10' CLG. VAULTED TO 13'

COVERED PATIO

BRKFT.
14X13
10' CLG. VAULTED TO 11'

FAMILY ROOM
23X18
10' CLG.

STOR.

MSTR. BDRM.
16X19
10' CLG.

BOOKS

STOR. BELOW STAIRS

LIVING RM.
15X17
CATHEDRAL CLG.
FROM 2 STORY HT.

14" BAR LEDGE

KIT
13X14

ENTERTAINMENT CENTER

SHOP AREA

PANTRY

MSTR. BATH
10' CLG.

STAIRS

HALL
10' CLG.

GALLERY ENTRY
12' CLG.

FORMAL DINING
12X14
10' CLG.

UTIL.

THREE CAR GARAGE

WALK-IN CLOSET

CHEST

NURSERY
(GUEST BDRM.)
12X14
10' CLG.

CHEST

COVERED PORCH

PLAN HPK2400098

First Floor: 3,168 sq. ft.
Second Floor: 998 sq. ft.
Total: 4,166 sq. ft.
Bonus Space: 210 sq. ft.
Bedrooms: 4
Bathrooms: 3½
Width: 90' - 0"
Depth: 63' - 5"
Foundation: Crawlspace, Slab, Unfinished Basement

ORDER ONLINE @ EPLANS.COM

Stucco corner quoins, multiple gables, and graceful columns all combine to give this European manor plenty of appeal. Inside, a gallery entry presents a formal dining room on the right, defined by elegant columns, while the formal living room awaits just ahead. The highly efficient kitchen features a worktop island, pantry, and a serving bar to the nearby octagonal breakfast area. The family room offers a built-in entertainment center, a fireplace, and its own covered patio. The left side of the first floor is dedicated to the master suite. Here, the homeowner is pampered with an octagonal study, huge walk-in closet, lavish bath, and a very convenient nursery. The second floor contains two family bedrooms, each with a walk-in closet, and a media area with built-in bookshelves.

HELPFUL HINT! Found a plan you *almost* love? A customization estimate for $50 is money well spent.

PLAN HPK2400099

First Floor: 2,469 sq. ft.
Second Floor: 1,786 sq. ft.
Total: 4,255 sq. ft.
Bedrooms: 4
Bathrooms: 4
Width: 66' - 8"
Depth: 69' - 3"
Foundation: Crawlspace

ORDER ONLINE @ EPLANS.COM

A stately brick facade expresses its traditional style with corner quoins, an arched entry, and keystone-topped lintels. Inside, an open floor plan accentuates the ease and flow from one room to another. Decorative columns add definition to the dining room and a fireplace and built-ins give the gathering room some warmth and charm. Double French doors introduce the patio, a perfect spot for enjoying the weather. The master suite also enjoys patio access and is further pampered by a large walk-in closet, dual-sink vanity, soaking tub, and shower enclosure. A guest suite or den can be found near the kitchen. Three family bedrooms each sport a walk-in closet and access to the second-floor recreation room and home office.

SECOND FLOOR

FIRST FLOOR

FIRST FLOOR

SECOND FLOOR

PLAN HPK2400100

FIRST FLOOR: 2,577 SQ. FT.
SECOND FLOOR: 1,703 SQ. FT.
TOTAL: 4,280 SQ. FT.
BEDROOMS: 4
BATHROOMS: 3½
WIDTH: 80' - 4"
DEPTH: 85' - 11"
FOUNDATION: CRAWLSPACE

ORDER ONLINE @ EPLANS.COM

Arched windows, soaring ceilings, and bright spaces make this resort-style home a dream come true. A grand entry opens to the formal foyer; to the left, the hearth-warmed study is both comfortable and dignified; ahead, the two-story great room encourages gatherings around the fireplace and expands out to the terrace through French doors. The dining room (with a wet bar), breakfast nook and sunroom are effortlessly served by the cooktop-island kitchen. The vaulted master suite enjoys abundant natural light and a luxurious spa bath. Upstairs, secondary suites are anything but inferior, with private or semiprivate baths, generous dimensions, and access to a sunken sitting room and a recreation room with a veranda.

PLAN HPK2400101

First Floor: 3,185 sq. ft.
Second Floor: 1,168 sq. ft.
Total: 4,353 sq. ft.
Bonus Space: 315 sq. ft.
Bedrooms: 4
Bathrooms: 4½
Width: 78' - 5"
Depth: 84' - 6"
Foundation: Unfinished
Basement

ORDER ONLINE @ EPLANS.COM

A medley of stone, brick, and stucco lends a European flavor to this home, while a thoughtful interior unites form and function in savvy rooms designed for comfort. Stately columns introduce a welcoming front porch. Inside, double doors lead to a quiet study that boasts a bow window, built-in cabinetry, and a stunning fireplace. At the heart of the home, the grand room features a gracefully curved two-story wall of windows and another fireplace. The gourmet kitchen provides plenty of counter and cabinet space and opens to both the keeping and breakfast rooms. The keeping room offers a lofty cathedral ceiling and a massive stone fireplace. The breakfast bay overlooks the rear covered porch and provides the perfect place for family meals. The master suite features a sitting bay anchored by a fireplace. Decorative columns set off this window-lined space from the homeowner's bedroom. Upstairs, three secondary bedrooms provide additional space for guests or family members. The optional bonus room easily converts to a fifth bedroom or exercise room.

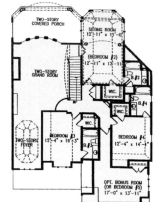

SECOND FLOOR

FIRST FLOOR

PLAN HPK2400102

FIRST FLOOR: 2,764 SQ. FT.
SECOND FLOOR: 1,598 SQ. FT.
TOTAL: 4,362 SQ. FT.
BEDROOMS: 4
BATHROOMS: 3½
WIDTH: 74' - 6"
DEPTH: 65' - 10"
FOUNDATION: CRAWLSPACE,
UNFINISHED WALKOUT BASEMENT

ORDER ONLINE @ EPLANS.COM

SECOND FLOOR

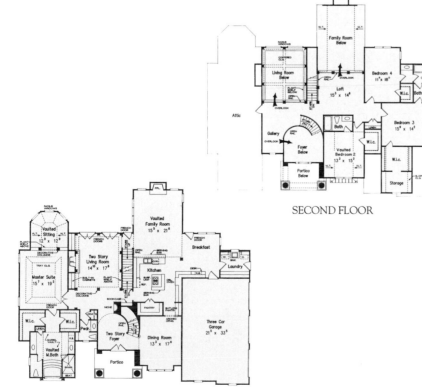

FIRST FLOOR

Greek-inspired portico columns and French Country rooflines make this home truly unique. At the heart of this magnificent design is the two-story living room with its fireplace and built-in bookshelves. To the right rear of the plan are the more casual rooms—the vaulted family room, island kitchen, and breakfast nook. A formal dining room, with kitchen access through the butler's pantry, awaits elegant meals at the front of the plan. The private master wing features a bayed sitting area and a deluxe vaulted bath with His and Hers wardrobes and vanity sinks. A curved staircase in the foyer gracefully winds its way up to the second floor. Here, three bedrooms, each with a walk-in closet, share two full baths, a loft, and a gallery that overlooks the first floor.

PLAN HPK2400103

FIRST FLOOR: 3,056 SQ. FT.
SECOND FLOOR: 1,307 SQ. FT.
TOTAL: 4,363 SQ. FT.
BONUS SPACE: 692 SQ. FT.
BEDROOMS: 4
BATHROOMS: 4½
WIDTH: 94' - 4"
DEPTH: 79' - 2"
FOUNDATION: CRAWLSPACE,
UNFINISHED BASEMENT

ORDER ONLINE @ EPLANS.COM

FIRST FLOOR

SECOND FLOOR

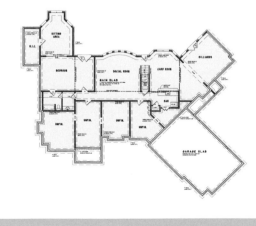

This fantasy begins as soon as you step from the porch into the two-story vaulted foyer. To the right sits the columned elegance of the formal dining room and to the left a personal library awaits. Steps away, the entrance to the master suite beckons with promises of a sitting area, morning kitchen, L-shaped walk-in closet, garden tub, separate shower, and dual vanities. The three family bedrooms upstairs each have a full bath and ample closet space. In addition to the bedrooms, the option of a game room/billiards room provides plenty of space for casual entertainment. A three-car garage completes this plan.

HELPFUL HINT!   Want to Mirror Reverse a design? It's an easy change to make for only $55.

FIRST FLOOR

SECOND FLOOR

PLAN HPK2400104

FIRST FLOOR: 3,121 SQ. FT.
SECOND FLOOR: 1,278 SQ. FT.
TOTAL: 4,399 SQ. FT.
BEDROOMS: 4
BATHROOMS: 3½ + ½
WIDTH: 86' - 7"
DEPTH: 81' - 4"
FOUNDATION: UNFINISHED BASEMENT

ORDER ONLINE @ EPLANS.COM

A brick/stone facade creates the solid exterior of this design. Inside, a library in the front is warmed by a fireplace, but the heart of the house is found in a large, open great room with a second fireplace. The spacious gourmet kitchen enjoys warmth from the grand room to the left and a third fireplace in the adjoining family room on the right. Access to a rear covered porch and deck/patio can be gained from the family room. There are three bedrooms upstairs and a bonus room/optional fifth bedroom. Each bedroom boasts a walk-in closet and convenient access to a full bath.

PLAN HPK2400105

First Floor: 3,297 sq. ft.
Second Floor: 1,453 sq. ft.
Total: 4,750 sq. ft.
Bedrooms: 5
Bathrooms: 4½
Width: 80' - 10"
Depth: 85' - 6"
Foundation: Slab

ORDER ONLINE @ EPLANS.COM

This elegant home combines a traditional exterior with a contemporary interior and provides a delightful setting for both entertaining and individual solitude. A living room and bay-windowed dining room provide an open area for formal entertaining, which can spill outside to the entertainment terrace or to the nearby gathering room with its dramatic fireplace. On the opposite side of the house, French doors make it possible for the study/guest room to be closed off from the rest of the first floor. The master suite is also a private retreat, offering a fireplace as well as an abundance of natural light, and a bath designed to pamper. The entire family will enjoy the second-floor media loft from which a balcony overlooks the two-story gathering room below.

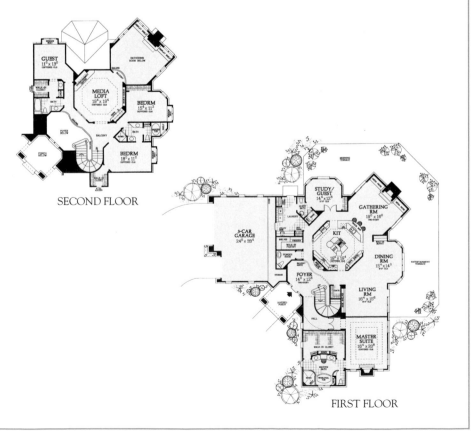

SECOND FLOOR

FIRST FLOOR

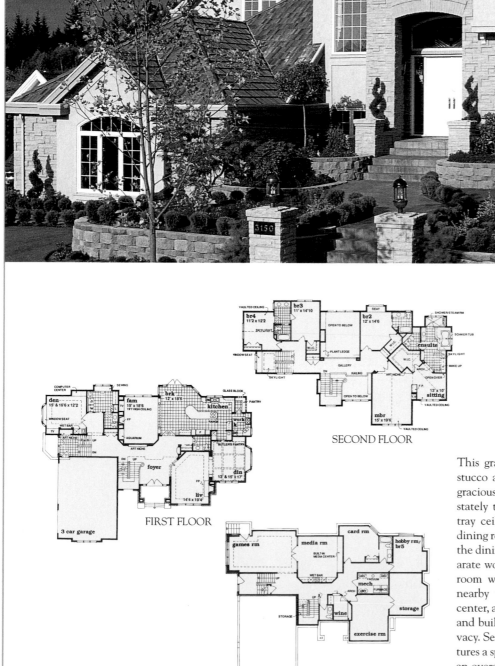

FIRST FLOOR

SECOND FLOOR

PLAN HPK2400106

FIRST FLOOR: 2,596 SQ. FT.
SECOND FLOOR: 2,233 SQ. FT.
TOTAL: 4,829 SQ. FT.
BEDROOMS: 4
BATHROOMS: 3½ + ½
WIDTH: 81' - 0"
DEPTH: 61' - 0"
FOUNDATION: Unfinished Basement

ORDER ONLINE @ EPLANS.COM

This grand, two-story home is adorned with a facade of stucco and brick, meticulously appointed with details for gracious living. Guests enter through a portico to find a stately two-story foyer. The formal living room features a tray ceiling and a fireplace and is joined by a charming dining room with a large bay window. A butler's pantry joins the dining room to the gourmet kitchen, which holds a separate work kitchen, an island work center, and a breakfast room with double doors leading to the rear patio. The nearby family room enjoys a built-in aquarium, media center, and fireplace. A den with a tray ceiling, window seat, and built-in computer center is tucked in a corner for privacy. Served by two separate staircases, the second floor features a spectacular master suite with a separate sitting room, an oversized closet, and a bath with a spa tub.

Colonial Comforts

A HISTORICAL ERA INSPIRES THE DESIGN AND AMBIANCE OF A NEOCLASSICAL HOME

This Neoclassical beauty takes a step back in time to the days of Washington and Jefferson. The symmetry of the columns, windows, rooflines, and chimney stacks are signature trademarks of this recognizable style.

From the foyer, a double staircase frames the entrance to a sunken living room with built-ins, a fireplace, and access to the rear porch. Four columns on the left define the kitchen where a snack bar provides a place for quick meals and a bayed eating nook access the patio with bar and grill. The dining room is also nearby for more formal occasions.

ABOVE: The home's U-shaped plan surrounds the backyard on three sides, forming a pleasant courtyard or a future pool location.
BELOW: A large pediment tops the four center olumns, an element typical of Colonial-era architecture.
OPPOSITE: Greek columns atop partial walls support the ceiling over the two-story foyer and great room.

RIGHT: Columns and steps divide the great room from the open kitchen and eating nook.
BELOW: The kitchen snack bar assures ample counter space while a nook beyond the oven offers extra cabinet storage.
OPPOSITE: The fully enclosed dining room has wall space for a china cupboard, buffet table, and full-length mirror.

On the other side of the home, a guest room lies at the front of the plan; in the back is the den and master suite. Enter the suite through the sitting room and step down into the sunken bedroom divided by a center fireplace. Continue to the left corner to find the master bath, where double vanities are respectfully placed in a nook away from the tub, shower, and compartmented toilet. The walk-in closet is large enough to share.

The second floor forms a half circle around the open living room, with one bedroom suite on each side. A balcony library, complete with a full wall of built-in bookshelves, also has an outdoor balcony porch. ■

ABOVE: A center-standing fireplace separates the cozy sitting room from the master bedroom.

FIRST FLOOR

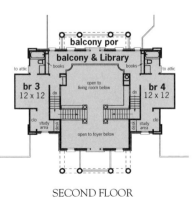

SECOND FLOOR

PLAN HPK2400107

FIRST FLOOR: 3,439 SQ. FT.
SECOND FLOOR: 803 SQ. FT.
TOTAL: 4,242 SQ. FT.
BEDROOMS: 4
BATHROOMS: 4 + 3 HALF BATHS
WIDTH: 95' - 0"
DEPTH: 90' - 0"
FOUNDATION: CRAWLSPACE, SLAB, UNFINISHED BASEMENT

ORDER ONLINE @ EPLANS.COM

HISTORICAL LUXURY

PLAN HPK2400108

FIRST FLOOR: 2,988 SQ. FT.
SECOND FLOOR: 1,216 SQ. FT.
TOTAL: 4,204 SQ. FT.
BASEMENT: 2,988 SQ. FT.
BONUS SPACE: 485 SQ. FT.
BEDROOMS: 4
BATHROOMS: 4½ + ½
WIDTH: 83' - 0"
DEPTH: 70' - 4"
FOUNDATION: CRAWLSPACE, UNFINISHED BASEMENT

ORDER ONLINE @ EPLANS.COM

SECOND FLOOR

FIRST FLOOR

Palladian windows, fluted pilasters, and a pedimented entry give this home a distinctly Colonial flavor. Inside, the two-story foyer is flanked by the formal dining and living rooms. The spacious, two-story family room features a fireplace, built-ins, and backyard access. A large country kitchen provides a work island, walk-in pantry, planning desk, and breakfast area. The lavish master suite offers a tremendous amount of closet space, as well as a pampering bath. A nearby study could also serve as a nursery. Upstairs, three bedrooms, each with a private bath, have access to the future recreation room over the garage.

HELPFUL HINT! The Right-Reading Reverse option flips the design but lets the on-plan text read correctly.

PLAN HPK2400109

First Floor: 2,081 sq. ft.
Second Floor: 940 sq. ft.
Total: 3,021 sq. ft.
Bedrooms: 4
Bathrooms: 3½
Width: 69' - 9"
Depth: 65' - 0"
Foundation: Walkout Basement

ORDER ONLINE @ EPLANS.COM

This Georgian country-style home displays an impressive appearance. The front porch and columns frame the elegant elliptical entrance. Georgian symmetry balances the living room and dining room off the foyer. The first floor continues into the two-story great room, which offers built-in cabinetry, a fireplace, and a large bay window that overlooks the rear deck. A dramatic tray ceiling, a wall of glass, and access to the rear deck complete the master bedroom. To the left of the great room, a large kitchen opens to a breakfast area with walls of windows. Upstairs, each of three family bedrooms features ample closet space as well as direct access to a bathroom.

SECOND FLOOR

FIRST FLOOR

QUOTE ONE®

SECOND FLOOR

FIRST FLOOR

PLAN HPK2400110

FIRST FLOOR: 1,455 SQ. FT.
SECOND FLOOR: 1,649 SQ. FT.
TOTAL: 3,104 SQ. FT.
BEDROOMS: 4
BATHROOMS: 3½
WIDTH: 54' - 4"
DEPTH: 46' - 0"
FOUNDATION: WALKOUT BASEMENT

ORDER ONLINE @ EPLANS.COM

The double wings, twin chimneys, and center portico of this home work in concert to create a classic architectural statement. The two-story foyer is flanked by the spacious dining room and formal living room, each containing its own fireplace. A large family room with a full wall of glass opens conveniently to the kitchen and breakfast room. The master suite features a tray ceiling and French doors that open to a covered porch. A grand master bath completes the master suite. Two family bedrooms share a bath and another has a private bath. Bedroom 4 features a nook for sitting or reading.

PLAN HPK2400111

MAIN LEVEL: 1,268 SQ. FT.
UPPER LEVEL: 931 SQ. FT.
LOWER LEVEL: 949 SQ. FT.
TOTAL: 3,148 SQ. FT.
BEDROOMS: 4
BATHROOMS: 3½
WIDTH: 53' - 6"
DEPTH: 73' - 0"
FOUNDATION: Finished Walkout
Basement

ORDER ONLINE @ EPLANS.COM

A covered front porch provides a welcoming entry for this Craftsman design, which features a stunning, amenity-filled interior. Vaulted ceilings adorn the great room, office, and even the garage; the dining room includes a built-in hutch, and the kitchen boasts a walk-in pantry. Upstairs, the master suite offers a walk-in closet with built-in shelves, along with a private bath that contains a spa tub; two additional bedrooms also have walk-in closets. A fourth bedroom, a recreation room with a fireplace and wet bar, and a wine cellar reside on the lower level.

MAIN LEVEL

UPPER LEVEL

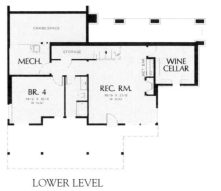

LOWER LEVEL

REAR EXTERIOR

PLAN HPK2400112

FIRST FLOOR: 1,388 SQ. FT.
SECOND FLOOR: 1,835 SQ. FT.
TOTAL: 3,223 SQ. FT.
BEDROOMS: 4
BATHROOMS: 3½
WIDTH: 37' - 6"
DEPTH: 78' - 5"
FOUNDATION: UNFINISHED
WALKOUT BASEMENT

ORDER ONLINE @ EPLANS.COM

Brick and siding blend seamlessly to inspire abundant curb appeal in this Craftsman home. Inside, the layout is equally seamless, incorporating a smart design. The kitchen easily serves the adjoining keeping room and breakfast nook. The screen porch and patio are ideal for entertaining and alfresco meals. Upstairs, the master suite, enhanced by stepped ceilings, boasts a lavish master bath and a private sitting area. Two additional family bedrooms are separated by a Jack-and-Jill bath. A computer station is conveniently located on this level. An exercise/media/guest room completes this plan.

FIRST FLOOR

Double Garage
21⁴ x 21⁴

Patio

Lnd.
11⁴ x 9⁰

Brkfst.
11⁸ x 11⁸

Keeping
12⁰ x 14⁸

Screen Porch

Kitchen
15⁶ x 15²

Living
17⁶ x 17⁴

Dining
15⁶ x 11⁶

Foyer

Lav.

SECOND FLOOR

Bath 3

Excercise / Media / Guest Rm.
16⁰ x 16⁴

Bdrm. 2
11⁴ x 13⁰

Bath 2

Sitting
11⁴ x 8⁸

Bdrm. 3
10⁶ x 12⁶

Master Bdrm.
17⁶ x 17⁸

M. Bath

PLAN HPK2400113

MAIN LEVEL: 2,293 SQ. FT.
UPPER LEVEL: 949 SQ. FT.
LOWER LEVEL: 1,088 SQ. FT.
TOTAL: 4,330 SQ. FT.
BONUS SPACE: 373 SQ. FT.
BEDROOMS: 3
BATHROOMS: 3½
WIDTH: 82' - 6"
DEPTH: 67' - 2"
FOUNDATION: Finished Walkout
Basement

ORDER ONLINE @ EPLANS.COM

MAIN LEVEL

UPPER LEVEL

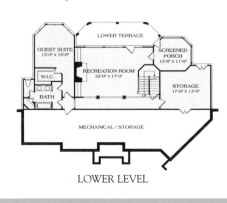

LOWER LEVEL

From its dramatic front entry to its rear twin turrets, his design is as traditional as it is historic. A two-story foyer opens through a gallery to an expansive gathering room, which shares its natural light with a bumped-out morning nook. A formal living room or study offers a coffered ceiling and a private door to the gallery hall that leads to the master suite. The dining room opens to more casual living space, including the kitchen with its angled island counter. Bonus space may be developed later.

HELPFUL HINT! Want to move the garage? Reverse the plan or modify it!

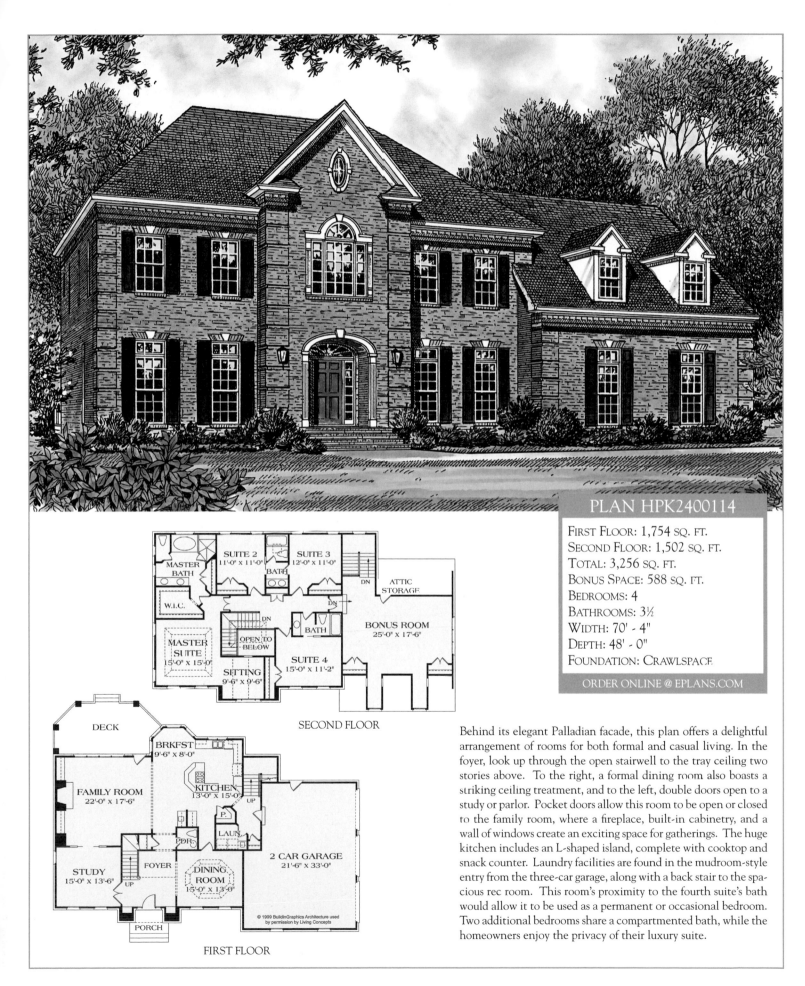

PLAN HPK2400114

FIRST FLOOR: 1,754 SQ. FT.
SECOND FLOOR: 1,502 SQ. FT.
TOTAL: 3,256 SQ. FT.
BONUS SPACE: 588 SQ. FT.
BEDROOMS: 4
BATHROOMS: 3½
WIDTH: 70' - 4"
DEPTH: 48' - 0"
FOUNDATION: CRAWLSPACE

ORDER ONLINE @ EPLANS.COM

SECOND FLOOR

- MASTER BATH
- SUITE 2 11'-0" x 11'-0"
- SUITE 3 12'-0" x 11'-0"
- BATH
- DN
- ATTIC STORAGE
- W.I.C.
- MASTER SUITE 15'-0" x 15'-0"
- DN
- OPEN TO BELOW
- BATH
- BONUS ROOM 25'-0" x 17'-6"
- SITTING 9'-6" x 9'-6"
- SUITE 4 15'-0" x 11'-2"

FIRST FLOOR

- DECK
- BRKFST 9'-6" x 8'-0"
- FAMILY ROOM 22'-0" x 17'-6"
- KITCHEN 13'-0" x 15'-0"
- UP
- P.
- LAUN.
- PDR.
- 2 CAR GARAGE 21'-6" x 33'-0"
- STUDY 15'-0" x 13'-6"
- FOYER
- DINING ROOM 15'-0" x 13'-0"
- UP
- PORCH

© 1999 BuildingGraphics Architecture used by permission by Living Concepts

Behind its elegant Palladian facade, this plan offers a delightful arrangement of rooms for both formal and casual living. In the foyer, look up through the open stairwell to the tray ceiling two stories above. To the right, a formal dining room also boasts a striking ceiling treatment, and to the left, double doors open to a study or parlor. Pocket doors allow this room to be open or closed to the family room, where a fireplace, built-in cabinetry, and a wall of windows create an exciting space for gatherings. The huge kitchen includes an L-shaped island, complete with cooktop and snack counter. Laundry facilities are found in the mudroom-style entry from the three-car garage, along with a back stair to the spacious rec room. This room's proximity to the fourth suite's bath would allow it to be used as a permanent or occasional bedroom. Two additional bedrooms share a compartment bath, while the homeowners enjoy the privacy of their luxury suite.

PLAN HPK2400115

FIRST FLOOR: 1,418 SQ. FT.
SECOND FLOOR: 1,844 SQ. FT.
TOTAL: 3,262 SQ. FT.
BEDROOMS: 4
BATHROOMS: 3½
WIDTH: 63' - 0"
DEPTH: 41' - 0"
FOUNDATION: CRAWLSPACE, SLAB,
UNFINISHED WALKOUT BASEMENT

ORDER ONLINE @ EPLANS.COM

Hipped rooflines, lintels, and French-style shutters give this home a taste of Europe. The two-story foyer is flanked by the formal living and dining rooms, and the living room opens through French doors to a private covered porch. A spacious, sunken family room features a warming fireplace framed by windows. The second floor has an overlook to the breakfast area and foyer. The lavish master bedroom provides a tray ceiling, a sitting room, a through-fireplace, and a sumptuous bath. Three family bedrooms and two full baths complete this level.

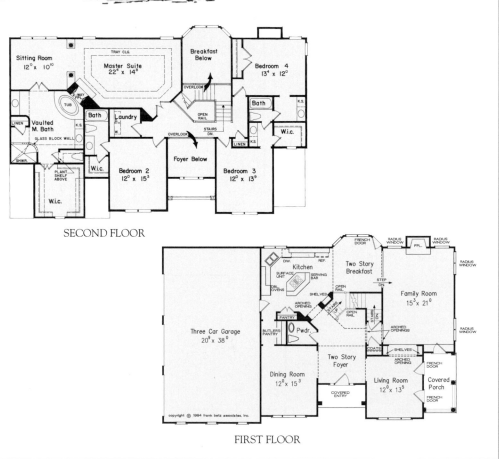

SECOND FLOOR

FIRST FLOOR

PLAN HPK2400116

FIRST FLOOR: 2,062 SQ. FT.
SECOND FLOOR: 1,279 SQ. FT.
TOTAL: 3,341 SQ. FT.
BONUS SPACE: 386 SQ. FT.
BEDROOMS: 5
BATHROOMS: 4½
WIDTH: 73' - 8"
DEPTH: 50' - 0"

ORDER ONLINE @ EPLANS.COM

SECOND FLOOR

FIRST FLOOR

A two-story chateau-style home may be exactly what you are looking for to entertain guests in grand style and accommodate a growing family. When visitors pass through the elegant columns on the front porch into the foyer with its spiral staircase and art niche, they know this is a special place. To the left is the formal dining room and straight ahead is the spacious, two-story-high great room with a centered fireplace flanked by built-in shelves. The huge kitchen with an island counter and handy pantry easily serves the dining room and the sunlit breakfast nook. The absolutely magnificent master suite assumes the entire right wing of the plan. Upstairs, four bedrooms (make one a study) and three baths offer plenty of comfort. A balcony overlooks the great room.

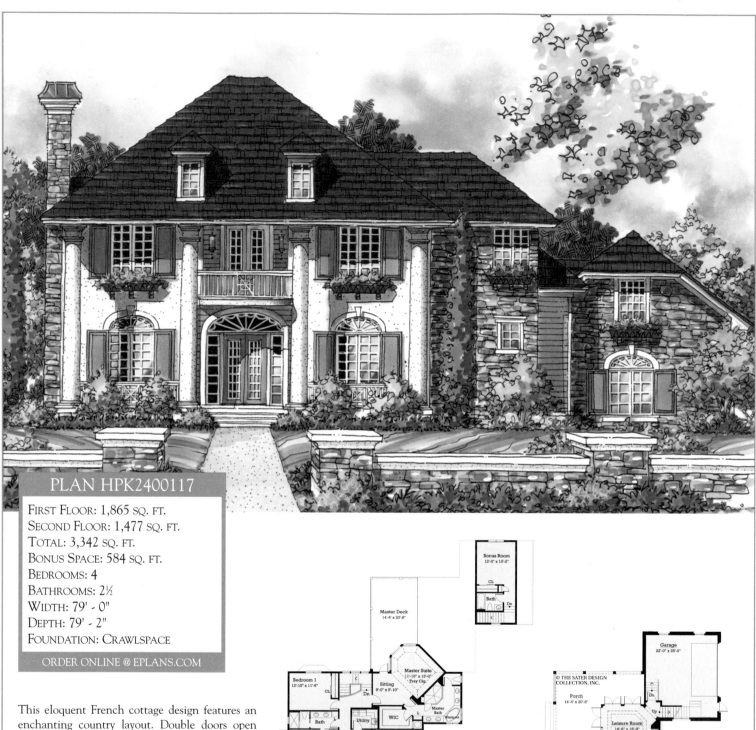

PLAN HPK2400117

FIRST FLOOR: 1,865 SQ. FT.
SECOND FLOOR: 1,477 SQ. FT.
TOTAL: 3,342 SQ. FT.
BONUS SPACE: 584 SQ. FT.
BEDROOMS: 4
BATHROOMS: 2½
WIDTH: 79' - 0"
DEPTH: 79' - 2"
FOUNDATION: CRAWLSPACE

ORDER ONLINE @ EPLANS.COM

This eloquent French cottage design features an enchanting country layout. Double doors open inside to a formal welcoming foyer. To the left, a living room is warmed by a fireplace, which connects to a bay-windowed study. A formal dining room is found to the right. The island kitchen opens to a nook and leisure room with built-ins. Three sets of double doors open onto the rear porch. Upstairs, the study hall opens to a romantic front balcony. Three family bedrooms share a hall bath. The master suite is an impressive retreat with a large sitting area accessing the master deck, a private whirlpool bath, and a huge walk-in closet.

SECOND FLOOR

FIRST FLOOR

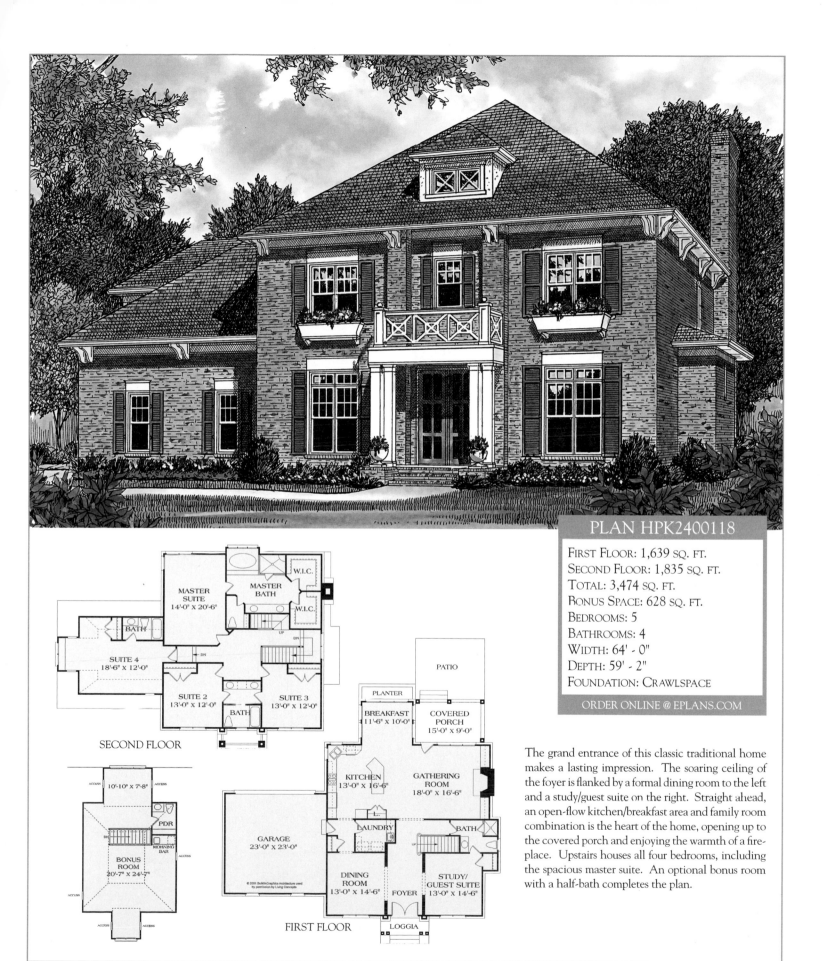

PLAN HPK2400118

FIRST FLOOR: 1,639 SQ. FT.
SECOND FLOOR: 1,835 SQ. FT.
TOTAL: 3,474 SQ. FT.
BONUS SPACE: 628 SQ. FT.
BEDROOMS: 5
BATHROOMS: 4
WIDTH: 64' - 0"
DEPTH: 59' - 2"
FOUNDATION: CRAWLSPACE

ORDER ONLINE @ EPLANS.COM

SECOND FLOOR

MASTER SUITE 14'-0" X 20'-6"
MASTER BATH
W.I.C.
W.I.C.
BATH
SUITE 4 18'-6" X 12'-0"
UP
DN
DN
SUITE 2 13'-0" X 12'-0"
BATH
SUITE 3 13'-0" X 12'-0"

ACCESS 10'-10" X 7'-8" ACCESS
PDR
DN
MORNING BAR
BONUS ROOM 20'-7" X 24'-7"
ACCESS
ACCESS
ACCESS

FIRST FLOOR

PATIO
PLANTER
BREAKFAST 11'-6" X 10'-0"
COVERED PORCH 15'-0" X 9'-0"
KITCHEN 13'-0" X 16'-6"
GATHERING ROOM 18'-0" X 16'-6"
GARAGE 23'-0" X 23'-0"
LAUNDRY
BATH
© 2001 BuildingGraphics Architecture used by permission by Living Concepts
DINING ROOM 13'-0" X 14'-6"
STUDY/ GUEST SUITE 13'-0" X 14'-6"
FOYER
LOGGIA

The grand entrance of this classic traditional home makes a lasting impression. The soaring ceiling of the foyer is flanked by a formal dining room to the left and a study/guest suite on the right. Straight ahead, an open-flow kitchen/breakfast area and family room combination is the heart of the home, opening up to the covered porch and enjoying the warmth of a fireplace. Upstairs houses all four bedrooms, including the spacious master suite. An optional bonus room with a half-bath completes the plan.

HELPFUL HINT! Want to hide the garage entrance? A minor plan modification may allow a side-load garage.

PLAN HPK2400119

FIRST FLOOR: 2,232 SQ. FT.
SECOND FLOOR: 1,269 SQ. FT.
TOTAL: 3,501 SQ. FT.
BEDROOMS: 4
BATHROOMS: 4½
WIDTH: 80' - 0"
DEPTH: 63' - 9"
FOUNDATION: Slab

ORDER ONLINE @ EPLANS.COM

In true Colonial style, this stately brick manor features large, bright windows; impressive columns; and stucco accents. Three entrances—a grand main portico, a side "friends'" porch, and a mudroom—cater to any occasion, welcoming family and guests. Encased in twin bay windows, a study and dining room enjoy elegant ceiling treatments. The two-story grand room is warmed by abundant sunlight and a fireplace framed by built-ins. The large family kitchen is joined by a bayed breakfast nook and an all-weather outdoor kitchen. In the master suite, a stepped ceiling and bay window embellish the bedroom; the bath has a walk-in shower and a corner whirlpool tub. Three upstairs bedrooms have private baths—Bedroom 2 and the guest suite offer private decks.

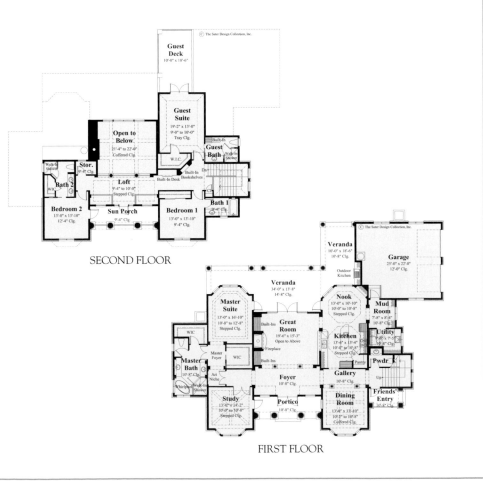

SECOND FLOOR

FIRST FLOOR

PLAN HPK2400120

FIRST FLOOR: 1,972 SQ. FT.
SECOND FLOOR: 1,533 SQ. FT.
TOTAL: 3,505 SQ. FT.
BEDROOMS: 3
BATHROOMS: 2½
WIDTH: 66' - 4"
DEPTH: 66' - 4"
FOUNDATION: Unfinished
Basement

ORDER ONLINE @ EPLANS.COM

SECOND FLOOR

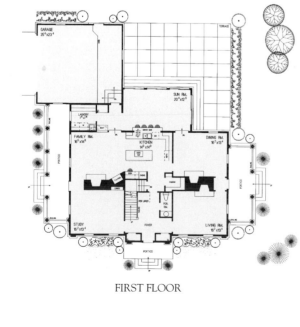

FIRST FLOOR

This dramatic residence, patterned after one built in 1759 by Major John Vassall in Cambridge, offers a floor plan that is intriguing in its wealth of amenities. On the first floor are the formal living and dining rooms, each with a fireplace. A front study connects to the family room with built-ins and another fireplace. Upstairs are three bedrooms, including a master suite with sitting room and deluxe bath.

PLAN HPK2400121

First Floor: 1,735 sq. ft.
Second Floor: 1,075 sq. ft.
Third Floor: 746 sq. ft.
Total: 3,556 sq. ft.
Bedrooms: 5
Bathrooms: 3½
Width: 64' - 0"
Depth: 64' - 0"
Foundation: Unfinished
Basement

ORDER ONLINE @ EPLANS.COM

Three floors of livability are available in this stately brick Federal design. From the two chimney stacks to the five dormer windows, the appeal is pure Americana. First-floor features include fireplaces in the gathering room, the breakfast room, and the study, as well as a built-in barbecue in the gourmet kitchen. A handy mudroom with a powder room connects the kitchen to the laundry and to the garage beyond. The second floor is dominated by a sumptuous master suite and two family bedrooms that share a full bath. A third floor holds two additional bedrooms that might serve well as guest rooms or as a studio or study space. A full bath with a double vanity finishes this floor.

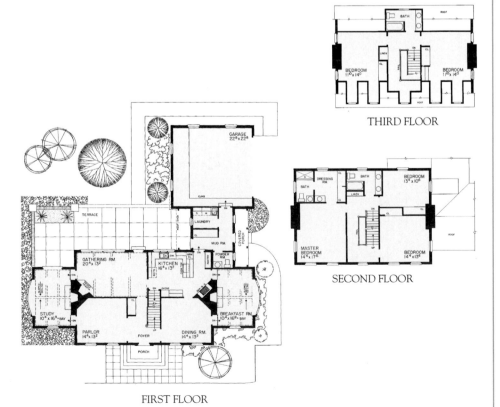

THIRD FLOOR

SECOND FLOOR

FIRST FLOOR

© The Sater Design Collection, Inc.

SECOND FLOOR

FIRST FLOOR

PLAN HPK2400122

FIRST FLOOR: 2,483 SQ. FT.
SECOND FLOOR: 1,127 SQ. FT.
TOTAL: 3,610 SQ. FT.
BONUS SPACE: 332 SQ. FT.
BEDROOMS: 4
BATHROOMS: 3½
WIDTH: 83' - 0"
DEPTH: 71' - 8"
FOUNDATION: SLAB

ORDER ONLINE @ EPLANS.COM

For a family desiring lots of outdoor living areas and an elegant interior, this French stucco manor is a place to call home. Formal areas at the front of the home welcome guests; ahead, the leisure room is bathed in light, an effect enhanced by the two-story ceiling. A two-sided fireplace here adds a cozy element. To the right, the study is stunning, with a beamed ceiling, built-in shelving, and shared heat from the fireplace. The country kitchen will please every member of the family, with plenty of counter space, room for a six-burner range, and an outdoor grill. The master suite is a resort on its own, featuring a bayed window, morning kitchen, enormous walk-in closet, and a sumptuous bath with a bumped-out whirlpool tub. Up the spiral staircase, three generous bedrooms, one with a private sun deck, share a bonus room.

© The Sater Design Collection, Inc.

PLAN HPK2400123

FIRST FLOOR: 2,484 SQ. FT.
SECOND FLOOR: 1,127 SQ. FT.
TOTAL: 3,611 SQ. FT.
BONUS SPACE: 332 SQ. FT.
BEDROOMS: 4
BATHROOMS: 3½
WIDTH: 83' - 0"
DEPTH: 71' - 8"
FOUNDATION: Slab

ORDER ONLINE @ EPLANS.COM

This appealing French Country design emphasizes effective indoor/outdoor relationships. A wide, welcoming front porch can be viewed from the living and dining rooms; to the back of the plan, the kitchen, leisure room, and study all open to the lanai. Upstairs, Bedroom 1 shares a balcony with the guest suite, while Bedroom 2 opens to a private deck. Other amenities include a fireplace shared by the living room and study; stepped ceilings in the living and dining rooms, kitchen, and study; and plenty of counter and cabinet space in the utility room. A vaulted bonus room above the garage offers room to grow.

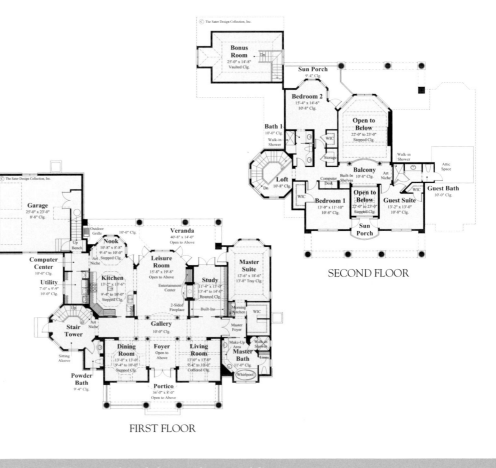

SECOND FLOOR

FIRST FLOOR

HELPFUL HINT! Head to ebuild.com for a wide array of doors, windows, lighting, cabinets, and flooring.

146   Order blueprints anytime at 1-800-521-6797 or eplans.com

PLAN HPK2400124

FIRST FLOOR: 1,450 SQ. FT.
SECOND FLOOR: 1,450 SQ. FT.
THIRD FLOOR: 730 SQ. FT.
BASEMENT: 1,676 SQ. FT.
TOTAL: 5,306 SQ. FT.
BEDROOMS: 3
BATHROOMS: 3 + 3 HALF BATHS
WIDTH: 38' - 0"
DEPTH: 82' - 0"
FOUNDATION: FINISHED WALKOUT BASEMENT

ORDER ONLINE @ EPLANS.COM

FIRST FLOOR

SECOND FLOOR

THIRD FLOOR

Beyond the understated entryway, a grand spiral staircase lifts the eyes up to the domed rotunda three floors above. Take the long way up or ride the built-in elevator from floor to floor. The master suite resides on the entry level, joined by a library, lounge, and conveniently located laundry room. Upstairs, an open great room, dining room, and kitchen find abundant space beneath an 11-foot ceiling. Outdoor living is offered at each level, but the third-floor terrace and media center are the home's main entertaining spaces. An outdoor fireplace allows year-round enjoyment.

PLAN HPK2400125

FIRST FLOOR: 2,421 SQ. FT.
SECOND FLOOR: 1,322 SQ. FT.
TOTAL: 3,743 SQ. FT.
BEDROOMS: 4
BATHROOMS: 3½
WIDTH: 66' - 9"
DEPTH: 63' - 0"
FOUNDATION: WALKOUT BASEMENT

ORDER ONLINE @ EPLANS.COM

This Colonial farmhouse inspires a sense of history, built to be cherished for generations to come. Inside, a two-story foyer opens to a quiet living room with a focal-point fireplace. The L-shaped kitchen overlooks a bright breakfast area with triple-window views and access to the covered rear porch and deck. A cathedral ceiling soars above the great room, which enjoys a warming hearth. The master suite with an oversized private bath nestles to the rear of the plan. A balcony hall on the second floor joins three family bedrooms—Bedroom 2 includes a private bath, while Bedrooms 3 and 4 share a full bath.

SECOND FLOOR

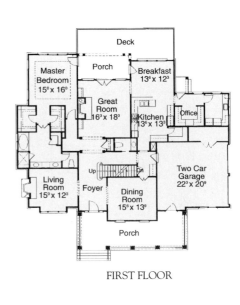

FIRST FLOOR

© The Sater Design Collection, Inc.

Veranda 20'-0" x 19'-7" Flat Clg.

Guest Suite 11'-8" x 16'-0" Flat Clg.

Outdoor Grille

Guest Bath

Storage

WIC

Leisure Room 18'-8" x 15'-9" Stepped Clg.

Game Room 12'-8" x 13'-11" Stepped Clg.

Sitting Area 10'-0" x 7'-11" Flat Clg.

Veranda 33'-11" x 14'-0" Flat Clg.

Nook 7'-0" x 9'-8" Flat Clg

Entertainment Center

Master Suite 16'-10" x 16'-9" Stepped Clg.

Pwdr.

Living Room 18'-9" x 13'-10" Coffered Clg. Fireplace Built-Ins

Kitchen 14'-0" x 16'-0" Stepped Clg. Pantry

Bedroom 2 12'-2" x 13'-0" Flat Clg.

WIC

Art Niche

Gallery

Window Seat

Bath 1 Walk-in Shower

Master Bath Flat Clg.

WIC

Study 11'-0" x 15'-10" Beamed Clg.

Foyer

Dining Room 12'-0" x 15'-2" Stepped Clg.

Utility 18'-6" x 10'-0"

Bedroom 1 12'-2" x 12'-0" Flat Clg.

Make-up Area Whirlpool

Walk-in Shower

Portico 9'-0" x 11'-5" Built-Ins

Garage 21'-0" x 37'-2" Flat Clg.

© The Sater Design Collection, Inc.

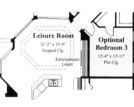

Leisure Room 21'-2" x 15'-9" Stepped Clg.

Optional Bedroom 3 12'-4" x 13'-11" Flat Clg.

Entertainment Center

FIRST FLOOR

PLAN HPK2400126

Square Footage: 3,790
Bedrooms: 4
Bathrooms: 3½
Width: 80' - 8"
Depth: 107' - 8"
Foundation: Slab

ORDER ONLINE @ EPLANS.COM

Grand chateau elegance was the inspiration for this magnificent European manor. Stone accents and detailed window treatments make this facade a masterpiece; inside, this family floor plan affords convenience and luxury. The living room greets you with a coffered ceiling, fireplace, and rear-property access. A study and dining room are on either side of the foyer, both brightly lit with natural light. In the gourmet kitchen, meal preparation is a breeze; ample counter space and a center island allow efficient culinary expression. The leisure room is defined by an entertainment center. The game room (with extra storage) can be finished for a third family bedroom. A guest suite is great for in-laws or live-in help. The master suite is a luxurious retreat, with a sitting room and gorgeous bath.

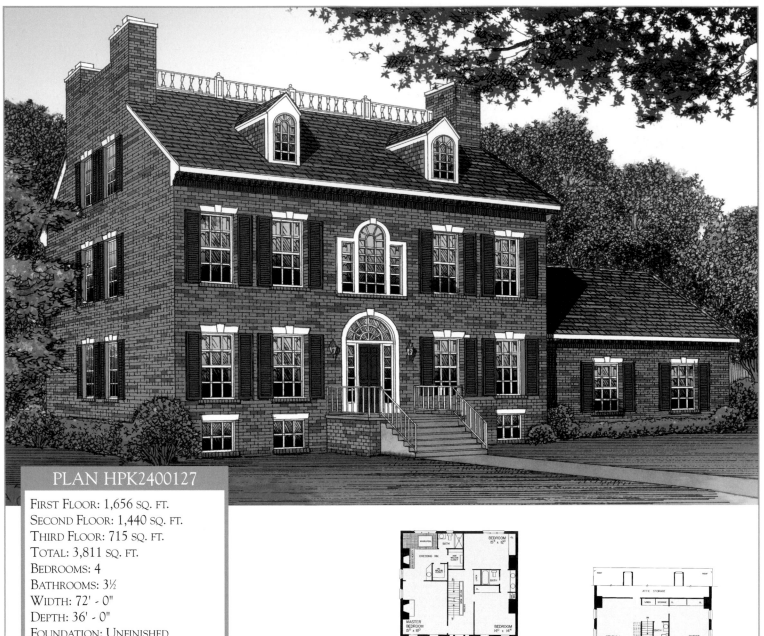

PLAN HPK2400127

First Floor: 1,656 sq. ft.
Second Floor: 1,440 sq. ft.
Third Floor: 715 sq. ft.
Total: 3,811 sq. ft.
Bedrooms: 4
Bathrooms: 3½
Width: 72' - 0"
Depth: 36' - 0"
Foundation: Unfinished Basement

ORDER ONLINE @ EPLANS.COM

This home recalls the home built by George Read II in New Castle, Delaware, around 1791. Its Georgian roots are evident in its symmetry and the Palladian window, keystone lintels, and parapeted chimneys. Notice, however, the round-head dormer windows, roof balustrades and arched front-door transom, which reflect the Federal styling that was popular at the end of the 18th Century. Three massive chimneys support six fireplaces, including one in each first-floor room and two in the master suite! The country kitchen also boasts an island cooktop, a built-in desk, a pantry, and sliding glass doors to the terrace. The second floor contains two family bedrooms, in addition to the luxurious master suite, while the top floor adds a fourth bedroom and a hobby/studio area. The garage includes an L-shaped curb for a work table and storage.

SECOND FLOOR

THIRD FLOOR

FIRST FLOOR

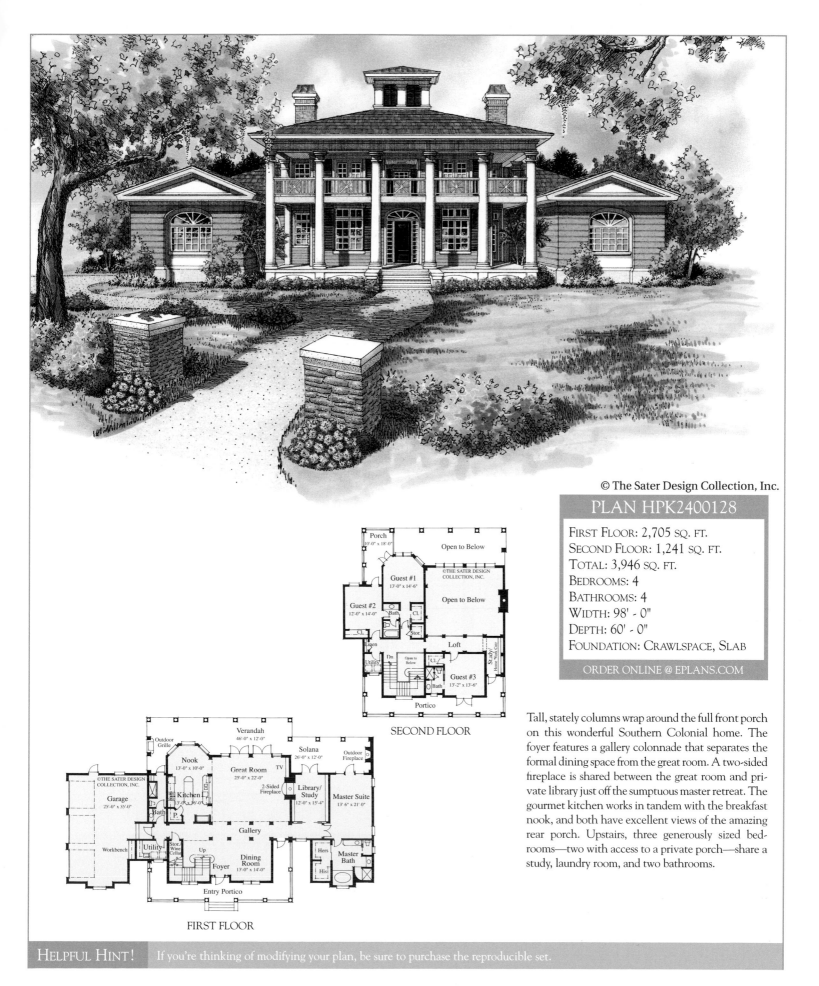

© The Sater Design Collection, Inc.

PLAN HPK2400128

First Floor: 2,705 sq. ft.
Second Floor: 1,241 sq. ft.
Total: 3,946 sq. ft.
Bedrooms: 4
Bathrooms: 4
Width: 98' - 0"
Depth: 60' - 0"
Foundation: Crawlspace, Slab

ORDER ONLINE @ EPLANS.COM

SECOND FLOOR

FIRST FLOOR

Tall, stately columns wrap around the full front porch on this wonderful Southern Colonial home. The foyer features a gallery colonnade that separates the formal dining space from the great room. A two-sided fireplace is shared between the great room and private library just off the sumptuous master retreat. The gourmet kitchen works in tandem with the breakfast nook, and both have excellent views of the amazing rear porch. Upstairs, three generously sized bedrooms—two with access to a private porch—share a study, laundry room, and two bathrooms.

PLAN HPK2400129

FIRST FLOOR: 2,126 SQ. FT.
SECOND FLOOR: 1,882 SQ. FT.
TOTAL: 4,008 SQ. FT.
BEDROOMS: 4
BATHROOMS: 2½
WIDTH: 92' - 0"
DEPTH: 64' - 4"
FOUNDATION: Unfinished
Basement

ORDER ONLINE @ EPLANS.COM

This historical Georgian home has its roots in the 18th Century. The full two-story center section is delightfully complemented by the one-and-a-half-story wings. An elegant gathering room, three steps down from the rest of the house, provides ample space for entertaining on a grand scale. The study and the formal dining room flank the foyer. Each of these rooms has a fireplace as its highlight. The breakfast room, kitchen, powder room, and laundry room are arranged for maximum efficiency. The second floor houses the family bedrooms. Take special note of the spacious master suite.

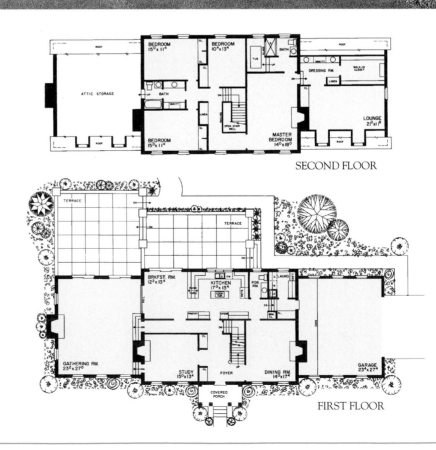

SECOND FLOOR

FIRST FLOOR

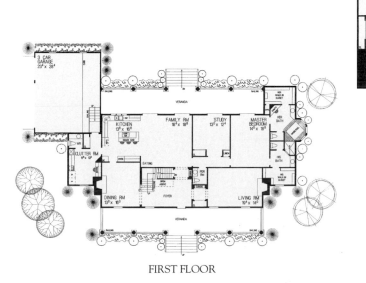

FIRST FLOOR

SECOND FLOOR

PLAN HPK2400130

First Floor: 2,658 sq. ft.

Second Floor: 1,429 sq. ft.

Total: 4,087 sq. ft.

Bedrooms: 4

Bathrooms: 5½ + ½

Width: 98' - 0"

Depth: 66' - 0"

Foundation: Unfinished
Basement

ORDER ONLINE @ EPLANS.COM

This antebellum Greek Revival manor represents the grace of Southern plantation style. Flanking a wide entry foyer are the formal living and dining rooms. Each has its own fireplace. Less formal activities take place in the family room, which is conveniently open to the island kitchen. A cooktop island with a snack bar serves both areas. A study separates the living areas from the master suite. The master retreat pampers the homeowners with His and Hers baths and walk-in closets. Three bedrooms and three baths occupy the second floor.

PLAN HPK2400131

FIRST FLOOR: 2,152 SQ. FT.
SECOND FLOOR: 1,936 SQ. FT.
TOTAL: 4,088 SQ. FT.
BONUS SPACE: 565 SQ. FT.
BEDROOMS: 4
BATHROOMS: 3
WIDTH: 104' - 4"
DEPTH: 57' - 10"
FOUNDATION: CRAWLSPACE,
UNFINISHED BASEMENT

ORDER ONLINE @ EPLANS.COM

In elegant Tudor style, this estate home has all of the best of luxury living. The vaulted foyer has a circular staircase and galleria above. The living room with a bay window and fireplace is on the left; a cozy den with double-door entry sits on the right. The dining room is defined by an arched opening and has a bay window, also. The U-shaped kitchen features a bar sink and bayed breakfast nook. Enter the sunken family room through decorative columns. You'll find a corner fireplace and sliding glass doors to the rear yard. The second floor holds four bedrooms—one of which is a master suite with a coffered ceiling and a private bath. Family bedrooms share a full bath.

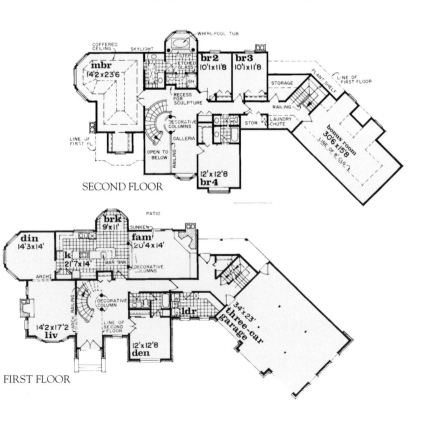

SECOND FLOOR

FIRST FLOOR

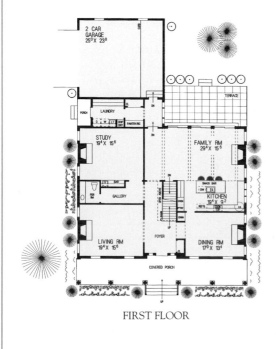

FIRST FLOOR

SECOND FLOOR

PLAN HPK2400132

FIRST FLOOR: 2,191 SQ. FT.
SECOND FLOOR: 1,928 SQ. FT.
TOTAL: 4,119 SQ. FT.
BEDROOMS: 4
BATHROOMS: 2½
WIDTH: 50' - 0"
DEPTH: 80' - 0"
FOUNDATION: UNFINISHED
BASEMENT

ORDER ONLINE @ EPLANS.COM

Covered porches upstairs and down are a charming addition to this well-appointed two-story Colonial home. Four chimneys herald four hearths inside: living room, dining room, family room, and study. The family room is enhanced by a kitchen snack bar for informal meals or interaction between guests and the cook. A rear patio can be viewed and accessed from here. The second floor holds four bedrooms. The master suite includes a warm fireplace, oversized walk-in closet, and relaxing master bath. Three family bedrooms share a full hall bath and a lounge with covered porch access.

PLAN HPK2400133

FIRST FLOOR: 2,807 SQ. FT.
SECOND FLOOR: 1,363 SQ. FT.
TOTAL: 4,170 SQ. FT.
BEDROOMS: 5
BATHROOMS: 3½ + ½
WIDTH: 109' - 4"
DEPTH: 47' - 0"
FOUNDATION: UNFINISHED
BASEMENT

ORDER ONLINE @ EPLANS.COM

Grand Georgian design comes to the forefront as semi-circular stairs approach an elegant front doorway flanked by arched windows. The foyer features a double stairway leading to the second floor, where four bedrooms share two full baths. Each of the front bedrooms has a walk-in closet with a window seat, and they share a sitting room overlooking the foyer. Downstairs, an impressive master suite features a luxurious bath and a private entrance to a study with a fireplace. Family members and guests will appreciate the gathering room with its fireplace and terrace access. To the left of the foyer, the dining room includes built-in corner cabinets, a traditional feature of Colonial homes. The roomy kitchen is a delight, with a work island, a breakfast nook, and a walk-in pantry. A four-car garage handles the largest of family fleets.

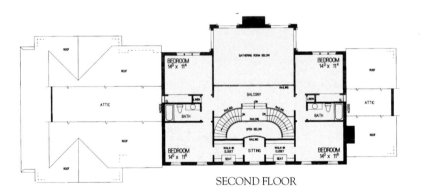

SECOND FLOOR

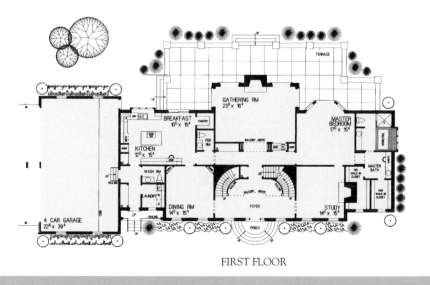

FIRST FLOOR

© William E. Poole Designs, Inc.

SECOND FLOOR

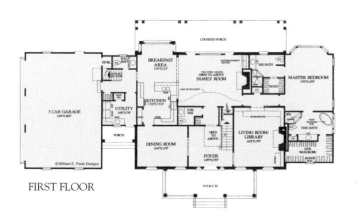

FIRST FLOOR

This fine example of the Georgian style of architecture offers a wonderful facade with Southern charm. The foyer is flanked by the formal dining room and the living room. The efficient kitchen is situated between the sunny breakfast nook and the dining room. The family room opens to the backyard. The master suite enjoys an opulent bath and large walk-in closet. The second floor presents three bedrooms and two baths.

© The Sater Design Collection, Inc.

PLAN HPK2400135

FIRST FLOOR: 2,163 SQ. FT.
SECOND FLOOR: 2,302 SQ. FT.
TOTAL: 4,465 SQ. FT.
BEDROOMS: 5
BATHROOMS: 5½
WIDTH: 58' - 0"
DEPTH: 65' - 0"
FOUNDATION: Slab

ORDER ONLINE @ EPLANS.COM

In true Williamsburg style, this stunning brick-and-stucco manor combines elegance and functionality for a perfect family home. Double doors open to reveal a foyer encircled by formal living areas. To the left, a library/study and gracious dining room enjoy vintage beamed ceilings. Ahead, the living room, defined by decorative columns, displays expansive views of the rear property. A full guest suite is great for frequent visitors. The country kitchen lies to the far right; here, an island and a bayed nook create a charming and efficient workspace. The leisure room is sure to be a family favorite. Not to be missed: the wine cellar, located behind the staircase. Upstairs, the master suite enjoys privacy and luxury. Three additional suites have private baths. All four generous bedrooms open to porches and balconies.

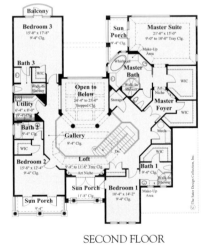

SECOND FLOOR

FIRST FLOOR

PLAN HPK2400136

MAIN LEVEL: 1,968 SQ. FT.
UPPER LEVEL: 1,056 SQ. FT.
LOWER LEVEL: 1,454 SQ. FT.
BASEMENT: 2,024 SQ. FT.
TOTAL: 6,502 SQ. FT.
BEDROOMS: 4
BATHROOMS: 4½
WIDTH: 34' - 0"
DEPTH: 74' - 0"
FOUNDATION: UNFINISHED BASEMENT

ORDER ONLINE @ EPLANS.COM

BASEMENT

LOWER LEVEL

MAIN LEVEL

UPPER LEVEL

The Victorian exterior is decorated with a balcony, arches, and a scallop trim. The foyer features a beautiful curved staircase and 20-foot ceiling height through the staircase. Each level of living space enjoys access to a deck to enjoy the outdoors. The master bedroom suite showcases a see-through fireplace and European-style master bath with spacious walk-in closet. The main level features an open-style living and entertaining space. The gourmet kitchen enjoys an oven cabinet, pantry, and island with sink and seating. The dining room is topped with a raised ceiling and the great room and library enjoy views to the rear and access to another deck. The top level offers a fourth bedroom, large entertainment area, and rooftop terrace and covered porch. An elevator offers easy access between floors and convenience for the homeowner.

PLAN HPK2400137

FIRST FLOOR: 2,968 SQ. FT.
SECOND FLOOR: 1,521 SQ. FT.
TOTAL: 4,489 SQ. FT.
BONUS SPACE: 522 SQ. FT.
BEDROOMS: 4
BATHROOMS: 4½ + ½
WIDTH: 82' - 6"
DEPTH: 81' - 8"
FOUNDATION: CRAWLSPACE

ORDER ONLINE @ EPLANS.COM

This home—showcasing elegant Georgian architecture—is reminiscent of the grand homes in the battery section of Charleston, South Carolina. The entry opens to the foyer with a grand staircase. To the right is the hearth-warmed library and to the left, the formal dining room. The foyer leads to the family room where a window wall looks out to the covered porch. A central hall passes the study and proceeds to the luxurious master suite, featuring a windowed tub and a huge walk-in closet. The left wing holds the sunny breakfast area, island kitchen, spacious mudroom, and garage. Upstairs, three bedrooms enjoy private baths and ample closet space.

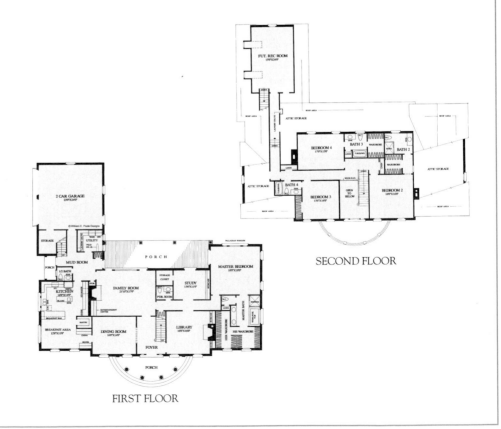

FIRST FLOOR

SECOND FLOOR

PLAN HPK2400138

FIRST FLOOR: 3,364 SQ. FT.
SECOND FLOOR: 1,160 SQ. FT.
BASEMENT: 2,414 SQ. FT.
TOTAL: 4,524 SQ. FT.
BEDROOMS: 4
BATHROOMS: 4½ + ½
WIDTH: 69' - 0"
DEPTH: 75' - 0"
FOUNDATION: BASEMENT

ORDER ONLINE @ EPLANS.COM

SECOND FLOOR

FIRST FLOOR

This imposing stone facade is full of grace and defined taste. An escalating front stairwell leads to elegant French doors. The two-story foyer is flanked by a dining room and study/retreat area—which is complete with a fireplace. A two-sided fireplace warms both the vaulted keeping room and the grand room, making entertaining a large group of guests entirely enjoyable. A butler's pantry is convenient to the dining room. The kitchen features a roomy island enabling serving to the keeping and grand rooms. The first floor also has two lavish master suites. Two family bedrooms, a balcony with a sun porch, two storage areas, and an optional bonus room are located on the second story, making this a home of luxury and practicality.

© William E. Poole Designs, Inc.

PLAN HPK2400139

FIRST FLOOR: 2,998 SQ. FT.
SECOND FLOOR: 1,556 SQ. FT.
TOTAL: 4,554 SQ. FT.
BONUS SPACE: 741 SQ. FT.
BEDROOMS: 4
BATHROOMS: 4½
WIDTH: 75' - 6"
DEPTH: 91' - 2"
FOUNDATION: CRAWLSPACE

ORDER ONLINE @ EPLANS.COM

The paired double-end chimneys, reminiscent of
the Georgian style of architecture, set this design
apart from the rest. The covered entry opens to the
columned foyer with the dining room on the left
and the living room on the right, each enjoying the
warmth and charm of a fireplace. Beyond the grand
staircase, the family room delights with a third fireplace and a window wall that opens to the terrace.
The expansive kitchen and breakfast area sit on the
far left; the master suite is secluded on the the right
with its pampering private bath. The second floor
holds three additional bedrooms (including a
second master bedroom), three full baths, a computer room, and the future recreation room.

FIRST FLOOR

SECOND FLOOR

SECOND FLOOR

FIRST FLOOR

PLAN HPK2400140

First Floor: 2,472 sq. ft.
Second Floor: 2,207 sq. ft.
Total: 4,679 sq. ft.
Bedrooms: 5
Bathrooms: 3½ + ½
Width: 80' - 8"
Depth: 52' - 0"
Foundation: Unfinished Basement

ORDER ONLINE @ EPLANS.COM

Recalling the grandeur of its Maryland ancestors, this manor house is replete with exterior details that make it special: keystoned lintels, fluted pilasters, a dormered attic, and a pedimented doorway. The centerhall floor plan allows formal living and dining areas to the front of the plan. Complementing these are the cozy library and large family room/breakfast room area. A service entrance off the garage holds a laundry room and wash room. Upstairs bedrooms allow more than adequate space. Over the garage is a complete guest apartment with living area, office, bedroom, bath, and kitchen.

PLAN HPK2400141

First Floor: 3,170 sq. ft.
Second Floor: 1,515 sq. ft.
Total: 4,685 sq. ft.
Bonus Space: 486 sq. ft.
Bedrooms: 4
Bathrooms: 3½
Width: 76' - 0"
Depth: 75' - 8"
Foundation: Slab

ORDER ONLINE @ EPLANS.COM

This modern Colonial home exhibits bold style and striking good looks. Historic details inside and out set the tone for a carefully designed plan with today's family in mind. Formal rooms at the front of the home welcome guests; to the rear, the family room basks in the sunlight of wide, tall windows. The well-planned kitchen is equipped with an island and walk-in pantry and extends into a breakfast bay that is surrounded with natural light. The master wing includes a bayed sunroom and lavish bath with a corner whirlpool tub. Three generous bedrooms, a craft room, and a future game room inhabit the second floor.

SECOND FLOOR

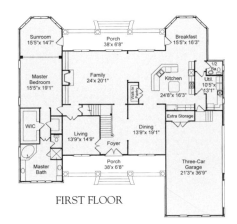

FIRST FLOOR

PLAN HPK2400142

MAIN LEVEL: 3,040 SQ. FT.
LOWER LEVEL: 1,736 SQ. FT.
TOTAL: 4,776 SQ. FT.
BEDROOMS: 5
BATHROOMS: 4½ + ½
WIDTH: 106' - 5"
DEPTH: 104' - 2"

ORDER ONLINE @ EPLANS.COM

MAIN LEVEL

LOWER LEVEL

Looking a bit like a mountain resort, this fine rustic-style home is sure to be the envy of your neighborhood. Entering through the elegant front door, one finds an open staircase to the right and a spacious great room directly ahead. Here, a fireplace and a wall of windows give a cozy welcome. A lavish master suite begins with a sitting room complete with a fireplace and continues to a private porch, large walk-in closet, and sumptuous bedroom area. The gourmet kitchen adjoins a sunny dining room that offers access to a screened porch.

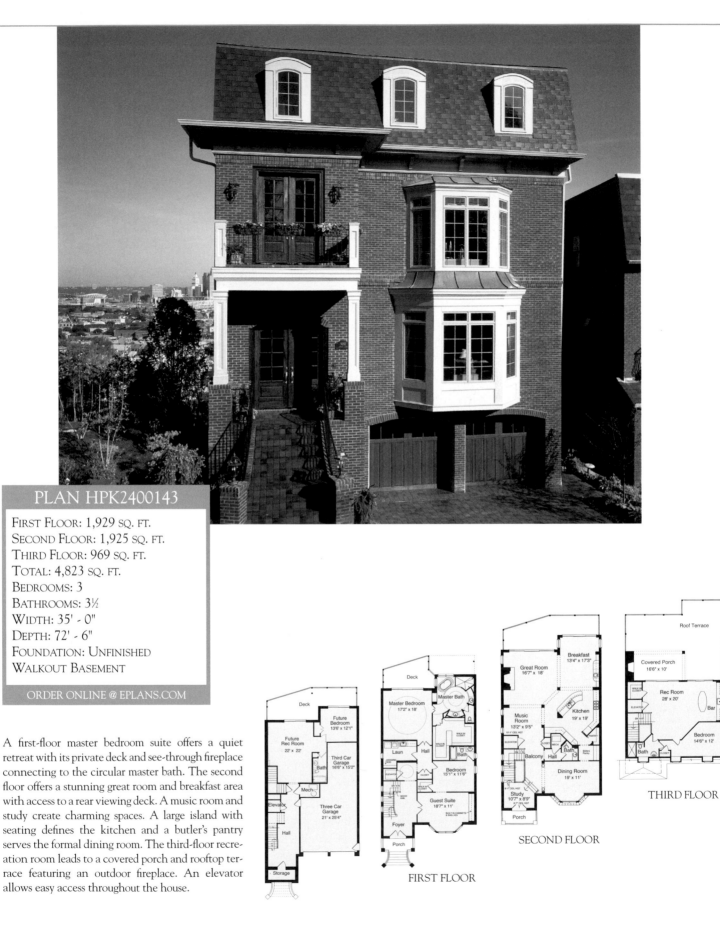

PLAN HPK2400143

First Floor: 1,929 sq. ft.
Second Floor: 1,925 sq. ft.
Third Floor: 969 sq. ft.
Total: 4,823 sq. ft.
Bedrooms: 3
Bathrooms: 3½
Width: 35' - 0"
Depth: 72' - 6"
Foundation: Unfinished
Walkout Basement

ORDER ONLINE @ EPLANS.COM

A first-floor master bedroom suite offers a quiet retreat with its private deck and see-through fireplace connecting to the circular master bath. The second floor offers a stunning great room and breakfast area with access to a rear viewing deck. A music room and study create charming spaces. A large island with seating defines the kitchen and a butler's pantry serves the formal dining room. The third-floor recreation room leads to a covered porch and rooftop terrace featuring an outdoor fireplace. An elevator allows easy access throughout the house.

FIRST FLOOR

SECOND FLOOR

THIRD FLOOR

HELPFUL HINT! We're the only plans seller with trained consultants available 24/7 to answer your questions.

PLAN HPK2400144

FIRST FLOOR 1,945 SQ. FT.
SECOND FLOOR: 1,945 SQ. FT.
THIRD FLOOR: 1,250 SQ. FT.
BASEMENT: 1,010 SQ. FT.
TOTAL: 6,150 SQ. FT.
BEDROOMS: 3
BATHROOMS: 2 + 3 HALF BATHS
WIDTH: 34' - 0"
DEPTH: 75' - 0"
FOUNDATION: FINISHED BASEMENT

ORDER ONLINE @ EPLANS.COM

BASEMENT

FIRST FLOOR

SECOND FLOOR

THIRD FLOOR

For a night of relaxation or to host a celebration, turn to this versatile urban design that embodies a graceful, festive spirit. The top floor features a wide-open layout and adjoining outdoor spaces that facilitate large social events. Guests will appreciate how the three-story design allows expansive views of the surrounding landscape. The second floor is a responsive living space for comfortable family gatherings. A rounded dining counter provides a casual alternative to the formal dining area, available at the rear of the level. At the front of the plan, two libraries and a comfortable great room provide quieter space. Luxurious sleeping quarters fill the first level of the home. The master suite includes generously proportioned and divided walk-in closets, as well as separate vanities. Private access to the rear deck from the master bedroom is an agreeable detail. Lastly, a walk-out basement allows a three-car garage and space enough for plenty of storage.

© Larry E. Belk Designs

PLAN HPK2400145

FIRST FLOOR: 3,276 SQ. FT.
SECOND FLOOR: 1,697 SQ. FT.
TOTAL: 4,973 SQ. FT.
BEDROOMS: 4
BATHROOMS: 4½ + ½
WIDTH: 106' - 2"
DEPTH: 77' - 10"
FOUNDATION: CRAWLSPACE, SLAB

ORDER ONLINE @ EPLANS.COM

This antebellum home evokes all the charm and elegance of the enchanting South. The two-story foyer opens to the formal living room and dining room. A nearby study features a spiral staircase to the game room upstairs. The kitchen is enhanced by a cooktop island and a breakfast bar. A double-sided fireplace serves the kitchen, breakfast room, and keeping room. Three family bedrooms—each with a private bath—are located on the second floor.

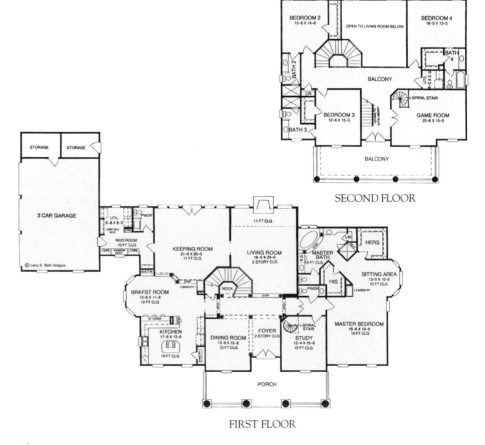

SECOND FLOOR

FIRST FLOOR

© Larry E. Belk Designs

SECOND FLOOR

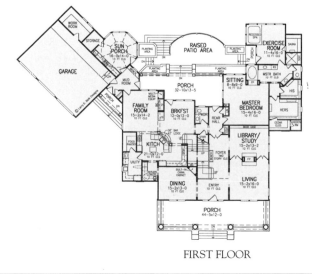

FIRST FLOOR

PLAN HPK2400146

First Floor: 3,253 sq. ft.
Second Floor: 1,747 sq. ft.
Total: 5,000 sq. ft.
Bedrooms: 4
Bathrooms: 4½
Width: 112' - 9"
Depth: 89' - 10"
Foundation: Crawlspace

ORDER ONLINE @ EPLANS.COM

This impressive two-story Craftsman design features a modern layout filled with abundant rooms and amenities. A wide front porch welcomes you inside to an entry flanked on either side by formal living and dining rooms. Built-ins enhance the dining room, while the living room shares a see-through fireplace with the library/study. The island kitchen offers a utility room and food pantry nearby, and it overlooks the breakfast and family rooms. The mudroom accesses the rear porch and sun room. The luxurious master suite contains a sitting area, His and Hers walk-in closets, a private bath, and an exercise room. At the rear, planters enhance the raised patio area. The second floor features three additional bedrooms. A study between Bedrooms 3 and 4 is perfect for the kids. A game room, sleep loft, and rear balcony complete this floor.

PLAN HPK2400147

FIRST FLOOR: 1,720 SQ. FT.
SECOND FLOOR: 1,740 SQ. FT.
THIRD FLOOR: 1,611 SQ. FT.
TOTAL: 5,071 SQ. FT.
BEDROOMS: 2
BATHROOMS: 2½ + ½
WIDTH: 45' - 0"
DEPTH: 60' - 0"
FOUNDATION: Unfinished
Walkout Basement

ORDER ONLINE @ EPLANS.COM

This stunning three-story home combines eclectic European style with modern amenities, all in a footprint small enough for an urban lot. The first floor is designed for recreation; a deluxe media room with tiered seating lies across from a billiard or exercise room, with a built-in wine rack tucked into the vestibule between. Guests will enjoy ultimate privacy in the bedroom suite on this level. The upper floors are accessible by two stairways and elevator, a priceless amenity for elderly or wheelchair-bound family members. On the second floor, a formal dining room is graced by a detailed ceiling; and the library sports a wall of custom built-ins. The kitchen features an oversized island, walk-in pantry, and an arched pass-through to the great room, which opens to a wide porch. Upstairs, the posh master suite includes a spa tub and over-sized walk-in shower. A partially-covered terrace and pub with wet bar provide myriad opporunities to relax and enjoy views of the city.

FIRST FLOOR

SECOND FLOOR

THIRD FLOOR

PLAN HPK2400148

First Floor: 3,170 SQ. FT.
Second Floor: 1,914 SQ. FT.
Total: 5,084 SQ. FT.
Bonus Space: 445 SQ. FT.
Bedrooms: 4
Bathrooms: 3½
Width: 100' - 10"
Depth: 65' - 5"
Foundation: Crawlspace

ORDER ONLINE @ EPLANS.COM

SECOND FLOOR

FIRST FLOOR

This elegantly appointed home is a beauty inside and out. A centerpiece stair rises gracefully from the two-story grand foyer. The kitchen, breakfast room, and family room provide open space for the gathering of family and friends. The beam-ceilinged study and the dining room flank the grand foyer, and each includes a fireplace. The master bedroom features a cozy sitting area and a luxury master bath with His and Hers vanities and walk-in closets. Three large bedrooms and a game room complete the second floor. A large expand-able area is available at the top of the rear stair.

PLAN HPK2400149

First Floor: 3,599 sq. ft.
Second Floor: 1,621 sq. ft.
Total: 5,220 sq. ft.
Bonus Space: 537 sq. ft.
Bedrooms: 4
Bathrooms: 5½
Width: 108' - 10"
Depth: 53' - 10"
Foundation: Slab, Unfinished Basement

ORDER ONLINE @ EPLANS.COM

A grand facade detailed with brick corner quoins, stucco flourishes, arched windows, and an elegant entrance presents this home. A spacious foyer is accented by curving stairs and flanked by a formal living room and a formal dining room. For cozy times, a through-fireplace is located between a large family room and a quiet study. The master bedroom is designed to pamper, with two walk-in closets, a two-sided fireplace, a bayed sitting area, and a lavish private bath. Upstairs, three secondary bedrooms each have a private bath and a walk-in closet. Also on this level is a spacious recreation room, perfect for a game room or children's playroom.

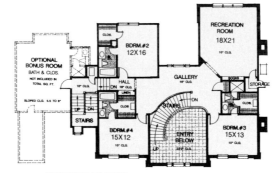

SECOND FLOOR

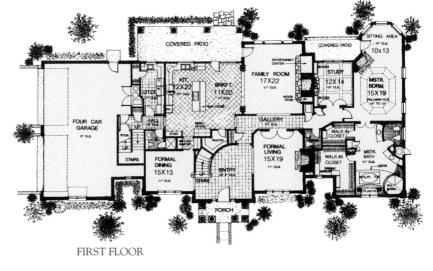

FIRST FLOOR

PLAN HPK2400150

FIRST FLOOR: 4,107 SQ. FT.
SECOND FLOOR: 1,175 SQ. FT.
TOTAL: 5,282 SQ. FT.
BONUS SPACE: 745 SQ. FT.
BEDROOMS: 4
BATHROOMS: 4½
WIDTH: 90' - 0"
DEPTH: 63' - 0"
FOUNDATION: UNFINISHED
WALKOUT BASEMENT

ORDER ONLINE @ EPLANS.COM

FIRST FLOOR

SECOND FLOOR

A sweeping central staircase is just one of the impressive features of this lovely estate home. Four fireplaces—in the library, family room, grand room, and master-suite sitting room—add a warm glow to the interior; the master suite, grand room, and family room all open to outdoor terrace space. There's plenty of room for family and guests: a guest suite sits to the front of the plan, joining the master suite and two more family bedrooms. Upstairs, a large bonus area—possibly a mother-in-law suite—offers a petite kitchen and walk-in closet; a full bath is nearby.

PLAN HPK2400151

FIRST FLOOR: 2,620 SQ. FT.
SECOND FLOOR: 2,001 SQ. FT.
THIRD FLOOR: 684 SQ. FT.
TOTAL: 5,305 SQ. FT.
BEDROOMS: 4
BATHROOMS: 5½ + ½
WIDTH: 67' - 0"
DEPTH: 103' - 8"
FOUNDATION: Crawlspace

ORDER ONLINE @ EPLANS.COM

THIRD FLOOR

SECOND FLOOR

FIRST FLOOR

With unique angles, brick detailing, and double chimneys, this home is as sophisticated as it is comfortable. The foyer enters into a refined gallery that runs past a dining room, complete with French doors opening to the front covered porch. The gallery also passes the grand room, which boasts a fireplace and three sets of French doors to the rear covered veranda. On the right, the master retreat provides its own private fireplace and access to the veranda. The kitchen and breakfast area are situated on the left side of the plan. Follow the steps up and an abundance of rooms will greet you. The recreation room directly accesses a small covered veranda. Two additional family suites flank the rec room, and each accesses a full bath. On the third level lies a 684-square-foot studio. A full bath and a balcony make this level a wonderful retreat.

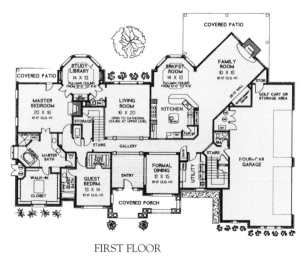

SECOND FLOOR

FIRST FLOOR

PLAN HPK2400152

FIRST FLOOR: 3,745 SQ. FT.
SECOND FLOOR: 1,643 SQ. FT.
TOTAL: 5,388 SQ. FT.
BONUS SPACE: 510 SQ. FT.
BEDROOMS: 5
BATHROOMS: 4½ + ½
WIDTH: 100' - 0"
DEPTH: 70' - 1"
FOUNDATION: CRAWLSPACE, SLAB,
UNFINISHED BASEMENT

ORDER ONLINE @ EPLANS.COM

Steep rooflines and plenty of windows create a sophisticated aura around this home. Columns support the balconies above as well as the entry below. An angled family room featuring a fireplace is great for rest and relaxation. Snacks and sunlight are just around the corner with the nearby breakfast room and island kitchen. A ribbon of windows in the living room makes for an open feel. A bay-windowed study/library has two sets of French doors—one to the living room and one to the master suite. The master bedroom offers a bath with dual vanities and a spacious walk-in closet. Three family bedrooms are located on the upper level with a recreation/media room and an optional bonus room.

PLAN HPK2400153

FIRST FLOOR: 4,193 SQ. FT.
SECOND FLOOR: 1,281 SQ. FT.
TOTAL: 5,474 SQ. FT.
BEDROOMS: 4
BATHROOMS: 4½ + ½
WIDTH: 94' - 0"
DEPTH: 71' - 0"
FOUNDATION: CRAWLSPACE, SLAB

ORDER ONLINE @ EPLANS.COM

A full-length receiving porch and second-floor veranda add Southern charm to this luxurious 5,474-square-foot home. With a grand winding staircase for a centerpiece, the home spreads outward with a master and guest suite, library, and formal dining room on the first floor, and additional guest suites and study on the second. From here you have a superior view of the family room below and through the immense windows leading to the rear veranda. Outside, robust columns support the roof that provides a secluded living space. Inside, they adorn the first floor in beautiful contrast to the delicate, carved railings of the staircase. A sitting room, His and Hers closets, and a double sink in the master suite, as well as a three-car garage and ample room for storage and amenities, give this home practical and aesthetic appeal.

REAR EXTERIOR

SECOND FLOOR

open to family room below

bath · wic · lin · attic
open to foyer below
dress rm · desk · down
br 3 17 x 16 · study · br 4 17 x 16
bath · wic · lin · str · attic
dress rm · desk
lad to attic
veranda

FIRST FLOOR

veranda

sitting 16 x 12 · fireplace
mbr 20 x 16
guest suite 14 x 13 · fireplace
family rm 26 x 22 · fireplace · built-in entertainment
breakfast
den 16 x 12 · fireplace
kit
bar
computer room
wic · bath · sto
his clo
her clo
dress
library 20 x 16 · foyer · dining 20 x 16
3 car garage 29 x 22
storage
receiving porch 50 x 8

© Larry E. Belk Designs

SECOND FLOOR

FIRST FLOOR

PLAN HPK2400154

FIRST FLOOR: 3,413 SQ. FT.
SECOND FLOOR: 2,076 SQ. FT.
TOTAL: 5,489 SQ. FT.
BEDROOMS: 4
BATHROOMS: 3½
WIDTH: 90' - 6"
DEPTH: 63' - 6"
FOUNDATION: UNFINISHED
BASEMENT

ORDER ONLINE @ EPLANS.COM

Classic design combined with dynamite interiors make this executive home a real gem. Inside, a free-floating curved staircase rises majestically to the second floor. The enormous living room, great for formal entertaining, features a dramatic two-story window wall. The family room, breakfast room, and kitchen are conveniently grouped. A large pantry and a companion butler's pantry serve both the dining room and kitchen. Privately located, the master suite includes a sitting area and a sumptuous master bath. The second floor contains Bedroom 2, which has a private bath. Bedrooms 3 and 4 share a bath that includes two private dressing areas. A large game room is accessed from a rear stair.

PLAN HPK2400155

First Floor: 3,545 sq. ft.
Second Floor: 2,019 sq. ft.
Total: 5,564 sq. ft.
Bonus Space: 928 sq. ft.
Bedrooms: 4
Bathrooms: 4½ + ½
Width: 124' - 4"
Depth: 79' - 3"
Foundation: Crawlspace,
Unfinished Basement

ORDER ONLINE @ EPLANS.COM

© WILLIAM E POOLE DESIGNS, INC.

SECOND FLOOR

FIRST FLOOR

This home provides a breathtaking example of the Neoclassical tradition. An impressive entrance is formed by an arched porch, fanned stairway, and columns. Upper and lower balconies, shuttered Palladian windows, a widow's walk, and a side-loading garage lend the exterior of this home its grandeur. The interior is replete with more columns, as well as tray ceilings, an indoor balcony, built-in cabinets and desks, and an entertainment center. The formal dining room comes with butler's pantry and leads directly off of the foyer for late-arriving dinner guests. A gallery and master study lead off in the opposite direction. The master suite of the main level holds a fireplace with private patio and deck access. Upstairs, find both front and sunset viewing decks. Three split bedrooms and special storage space round out the surprise of the upper floor.

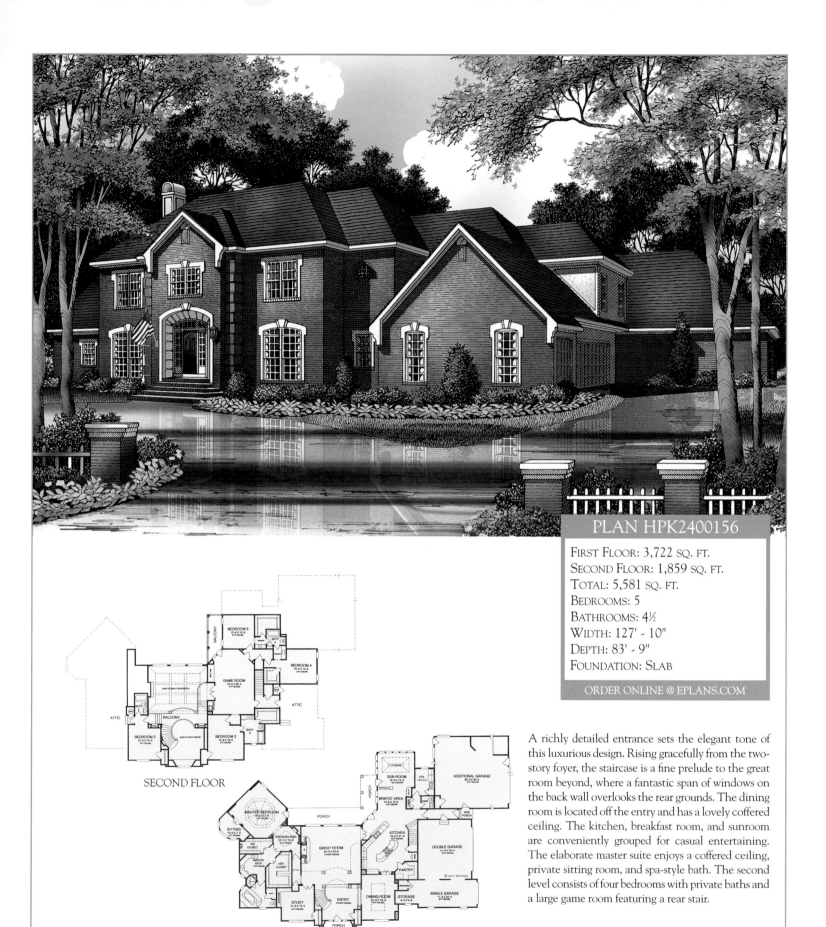

PLAN HPK2400156

First Floor: 3,722 sq. ft.
Second Floor: 1,859 sq. ft.
Total: 5,581 sq. ft.
Bedrooms: 5
Bathrooms: 4½
Width: 127' - 10"
Depth: 83' - 9"
Foundation: Slab

ORDER ONLINE @ EPLANS.COM

SECOND FLOOR

FIRST FLOOR

A richly detailed entrance sets the elegant tone of this luxurious design. Rising gracefully from the two-story foyer, the staircase is a fine prelude to the great room beyond, where a fantastic span of windows on the back wall overlooks the rear grounds. The dining room is located off the entry and has a lovely coffered ceiling. The kitchen, breakfast room, and sunroom are conveniently grouped for casual entertaining. The elaborate master suite enjoys a coffered ceiling, private sitting room, and spa-style bath. The second level consists of four bedrooms with private baths and a large game room featuring a rear stair.

PLAN HPK2400157

First Floor: 3,669 sq. ft.
Second Floor: 2,048 sq. ft.
Total: 5,717 sq. ft.
Bonus Space: 375 sq. ft.
Bedrooms: 5
Bathrooms: 4½ + ½
Width: 108' - 10"
Depth: 72' - 0"
Foundation: Crawlspace

ORDER ONLINE @ EPLANS.COM

A massive pillared portico bids entry into this stunning two-story. While a formal dining room and a quiet study flank the foyer, a dramatic sweeping staircase takes center stage. Beyond it is a columned grand room with a fireplace and access to the rear terrace. A gourmet island kitchen with a large walk-in pantry provides access to the dining room via a butler's pantry or to the breakfast nook and the secluded family room with its central fireplace. The master suite commands the right wing of the home and features terrace access and an opulent master bath with separate walk-in closets and a whirlpool tub. Four family bedrooms and three full baths are available upstairs, as well as bonus space that can be made into a studio or a game room.

SECOND FLOOR

FIRST FLOOR

PLAN HPK2400158

MAIN LEVEL: 4,011 SQ. FT.
UPPER LEVEL: 2,198 SQ. FT.
LOWER LEVEL: 3,071 SQ. FT.
TOTAL: 6,209 SQ. FT.
BEDROOMS: 4
BATHROOMS: 3½ + ½
WIDTH: 136' - 0"
DEPTH: 69' - 2"
FOUNDATION: UNFINISHED
WALKOUT BASEMENT

ORDER ONLINE @ EPLANS.COM

MAIN LEVEL

UPPER LEVEL

LOWER LEVEL

This magnificent Southern-style mansion offers all the features needed for graceful entertaining and refined living. From the stately columns that welcome visitors at the entry to the splendid spiral stairway winding up to the second level, this home is stunning. An octagonal library towards the front guarantees private quietude. An expansive deck with a covered porch at one end and a pampering hot tub at the other will bring hours of enjoyment. Fantastic meals can be prepared in the spacious country kitchen. A resplendent master suite on the main floor enjoys a roomy dressing area; upstairs, three more bedrooms, one of them a posh guest suite, offer delightful sleeping accommodations. In addition to the formal dining area and impressive hearth room, the first floor also enjoys a music room and a convenient mudroom.

HELPFUL HINT! The national cost-to-build average, based on the heated living space of the home, is $110 per sq. ft.

Luxury
Built From The Ground Up

Hanley Wood offers the largest selection of plans, from the nation's hottest designers. With titles to satisfy every taste and plans to suit the most demanding customers, our plan books are essential for every builder's collections.

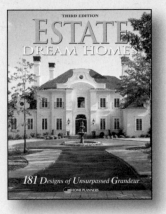

Estate Dream Homes, 3rd Ed.

Twenty-one of the most respected names in residential architecture have pooled their talents to bring 181 pre-designed custom home plans to the public. Designs include lavish amenities and styles from all regions of the country.

$16.95 U.S.
ISBN-10: 1-931131-00-7
224 pages (32 full-color)

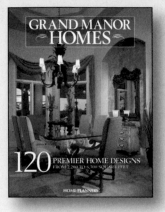

Grand Manor Homes

This collection of 120 premier designs brings a new perspective of what upscale design can be. From Country to European, these plans offer opulent interior features and abundant outdoor space.

$17.95 U.S.
ISBN-10: 1-931131-17-1
192 full-color pages

NEW!

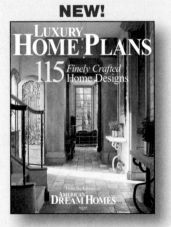

Luxury Home Plans

Explore this carefully chosen collection of the most luxurious, high-end homes dotting America's landscape. Featured home plans provide an inside look at custom details and elegant decor, and the unique amenities offered in these opulent plans.

$19.95 U.S.
ISBN-10: 1-931131-63-5
ISBN-13: 978-1-931131-63-6
192 pages

NEW!

Big Book of Designer Home Plans

This fabulous compilation profiles ten top designers and reveals dozens of their most popular home plans.

$12.95 U.S.
ISBN-10: 1-931131-68-6
ISBN-13: 978-1-931131-68-1
464 pages

Hanley Wood Books

One Thomas Circle, NW | Suite 600 | Washington, DC 20005
877.447.5450 | www.hanleywoodbooks.com

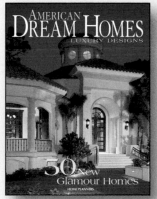

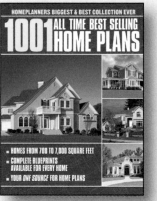

Offering your customers elegance and style has never been easier. Hanley Wood's array of luxury titles deliver the distinctive plans that will capture your customers' imaginations. Our plan books are essential for every builder's collections.

American Dream Homes

These portfolios of innovative luxury designs, from classic to cutting edge, feature courtyards, sculpted spaces, and tech-savvy style. The grand, yet highly livable retreats satisfy even the most demanding homeowners.

$19.95 U.S.
ISBN-10: 1-931131-08-2
256 pages

1001 All Time Best Selling Home Plans

The largest compendium available, with complete blueprints for every style of home — from Tudor to Southwestern, Contemporary to Victorian, this book has it all.

$12.95 U.S.
ISBN-10: 1-881955-67-2
704 pages (32 full-color)

If your customers are looking for luxury—make sure they look no further.

With more than 50 years of experience in the industry and millions of blueprints sold, Hanley Wood is a trusted source of high-quality, high-value pre-drawn home plans.

Using pre-drawn home plans is a **reliable, cost-effective way** to build your dream home, and our vast selection of plans is second-to-none. The nation's finest designers craft these plans that builders know they can trust. Meanwhile, our friendly, knowledgeable customer service representatives can help you every step of the way.

WHAT YOU'LL GET WITH YOUR ORDER

The contents of each designer's blueprint package is unique, but all contain detailed, high-quality working drawings. You can expect to find the following standard elements in most sets of plans:

I. FRONT PERSPECTIVE

This artist's sketch of the exterior of the house gives you an idea of how the house will look when built and landscaped.

2. FOUNDATION AND BASEMENT PLANS

This sheet shows the foundation layout including concrete walls, footings, pads, posts, beams, bearing walls, and foundation notes. If the home features a basement, the first-floor framing details may also be included on this plan. If your plan features slab construction rather than a basement, the plan shows footings and details for a monolithic slab. This page, or another in the set, may include a sample plot plan for locating your house on a building site. Additional sheets focus on foundation cross-sections and other details.

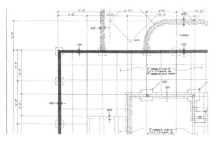

3. DETAILED FLOOR PLANS

These plans show the layout of each floor of the house. Rooms and interior spaces are carefully dimensioned, doors and windows located, and keys are given for cross-section details provided elsewhere in the plans.

4. HOUSE AND DETAIL CROSS-SECTIONS

Large-scale views show sections or cutaways of the foundation, interior walls, exterior walls, floors, stairways, and roof details. Additional cross-sections may show important changes in floor, ceiling, or roof heights, or the relationship of one level to another. These sections show exactly how the various parts of the house fit together and are extremely valuable during construction. Additional sheets may include enlarged wall, floor, and roof construction details.

5. FLOOR STRUCTURAL SUPPORTS

The floor framing plans provide detail for these crucial elements of your home. Each includes floor joist, ceiling joist, spacing, direction, span, and specifications. Beam and window headers, along with necessary details for framing connections, stairways, or dormers are also included.

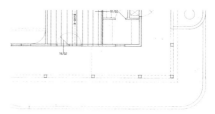

6. ELECTRICAL PLAN

The electrical plan offers suggested locations with notes for all lighting, outlets, switches, and circuits. A layout is provided for each level, as well as basements, garages, or other structures. This plan does not contain diagrams detailing how all wiring should be run, or how circuits should be engineered. These details should be designed by your electrician.

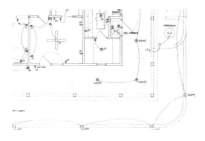

7. EXTERIOR ELEVATIONS

In addition to the front exterior, your blueprint set will include drawings of the rear and sides of your house as well. These drawings give notes on exterior materials and finishes. Particular attention is given to cornice detail, brick and stone accents, or other finish items that make your home unique.

ROOF FRAMING PLANS — PLEASE READ

Some plans contain roof framing plans; however because of the wide variation in local requirements, many plans do not. If you buy a plan without a roof framing plan, you will need an engineer familiar with local building codes to create a plan to build your roof. Even if your plan does contain a roof framing plan, we recommend that a local engineer review the plan to verify that it will meet local codes.

BEFORE YOU CALL

You are making a terrific decision to use a pre-drawn house plan—it is one you can make with confidence, knowing that your blueprints are crafted by national-award-winning certified residential designers and architects, and trusted by builders.

Once you've selected the plan you want—or even if you have questions along the way—our experienced customer service representatives are available 24 hours a day, seven days a week to help you navigate the home-building process. To help them provide you with even better service, please consider the following questions before you call:

■ **Have you chosen or purchased your lot?**
If so, please review the building setback requirements of your local building authority before you call. You don't need to have a lot before ordering plans, but if you own land already, please have the width and depth dimensions handy when you call.

■ **Have you chosen a builder?**
Involving your builder in the plan selection and evaluation process may be beneficial. Luckily, builders know they can have confidence with pre-drawn plans because they've been designed for livability, functionality, and typically are builder-proven at successful home sites across the country.

■ **Do you need a construction loan?**
Construction loans are unique because they involve determining the value of something that is not yet constructed. Several lenders offer convenient contstruction-to-permanent loans. It is important to choose a good lending partner—one who will help guide you through the application and appraisal process. Most will even help you evaluate your contractor to ensure reliability and credit worthiness. Our partnership with IndyMac Bank, a nationwide leader in construction loans, can help you save on your loan, if needed (see the next page for details).

■ **How many sets of plans do you need?**
Building a home can typically require a number of sets of blueprints—one for yourself, two or three for the builder and subcontractors, two for the local building department, and one or

more for your lender. For this reason, we offer 5- and 8-set plan packages, but your best value is the Reproducible Plan Package. Reproducible plans are accompanied by a license to make modifications and typically up to 12 duplicates of the plan so you have enough copies of the plan for everyone involved in the financing and construction of your home.

■ **Do you want to make any changes to the plan?**
We understand that it is difficult to find blueprints for a home that will meet all of your needs. That is why Hanley Wood is glad to offer plan Customization Services. We will work with you to design the modifications you'd like to see and to adjust your blueprint plans accordingly—anything from changing the foundation; adding square footage, redesigning baths, kitchens, or bedrooms; or most other modifications. This simple, cost-effective service saves you from hiring an outside architect to make alterations. Modifications may only be made to Reproducible Plan Packages that include the license to modify.

■ **Do you have to make any changes to meet local building codes?**
While all of our plans are drawn to meet national building codes at the time they were created, many areas required that plans be stamped by a local engineer to certify that they meet local building codes. Building codes are updated frequently and can vary by state, county, city, or municipality. Contact your local building inspection department, office of planning and zoning, or department of permits to determine how your local codes will affect your construction project. The best way to assure that you can make changes to your plan, if necessary, is to purchase a Reproducible Plan Package.

■ **Has everyone—from family members to contractors—been involved in selecting the plan?**
Building a new home is an exciting process, and using pre-drawn plans is a great way to realize your dreams. Make sure that everyone involved has had an opportunity to review the plan you've selected. While Hanley Wood is the only plans provider with an exchange policy, it's best to be sure all parties agree on your selection before you buy.

CALL TOLL-FREE 1-800-521-6797

Source Key
HPK24

CUSTOMIZE YOUR PLAN –
HANLEY WOOD CUSTOMIZATION SERVICES

Creating custom home plans has never been easier and more directly accessible. Using state-of-the-art technology and top-performing architectural expertise, Hanley Wood delivers on a long-standing customer commitment to provide world-class home-plans and customization services. Our valued customers—professional home builders and individual home owners—appreciate the convenience and accessibility of this interactive, consultative service.

With the Hanley Wood Customization Service you can:
■ Save valuable time by avoiding drawn-out and frequently repetitive face-to-face design meetings

■ Communicate design and home-plan changes faster and more efficiently
■ Speed-up project turn-around time
■ Build on a budget without sacrificing quality
■ Transform master home plans to suit your design needs and unique personal style

All of our design options and prices are impressively affordable. A detailed quote is available for a $50 consultation fee. Plan modification is an interactive service. Our skilled team of designers will guide you through the customization process from start to finish making recommendations, offering ideas, and determining the feasibility of your changes. This level of service is offered to ensure the final modified plan meets your expectations. If you use our service the $50 fee will be applied to the cost of the modifications.

You may purchase the customization consultation before or after purchasing a plan. In either case, it is necessary to purchase the Reproducible Plan Package and complete the accompanying license to modify the plan before we can begin customization.

Customization Consultation **$50**

TOOLS TO WORK WITH YOUR BUILDER

Two Reverse Options For Your Convenience – Mirror and Right-Reading Reverse (as available)
Mirror reverse plans simply flip the design 180 degrees—keep in mind, the text will also be flipped. For a minimal fee you can have one or all of your plans shipped mirror reverse, although we recommend having at least one regular set handy. Right-reading reverse plans show the design flipped 180 degrees but the text reads normally. When you choose this option, we ship each set of purchased blueprints in this format.

Mirror Reverse Fee (indicate the number of sets when ordering) $55
Right Reading Reverse Fee (all sets are reversed) $175

A Shopping List Exclusively for Your Home – Materials List
A customized Materials List helps you plan and estimate the cost of your new home, outlining the quantity, type, and size of materials needed to build your house (with the exception of mechanical system items). Included are framing lumber, windows and doors, kitchen and bath cabinetry, rough and finished hardware, and much more.

Materials List . . . .**$85 each**
Additional Materials Lists (at original time of purchase only)$20 each

Plan Your Home-Building Process – Specification Outline
Work with your builder on this step-by-step chronicle of 166 stages or items crucial to the building process. It provides a comprehensive review of the construction process and helps you choose materials.
Specification Outline . . . .**$10 each**

Get Accurate Cost Estimates for Your Home – Quote One® Cost Reports
The Summary Cost Report, the first element in the Quote One® package, breaks down the cost of your home into various categories based on building materials, labor, and installation, and includes three grades of construction: Budget, Standard, and Custom. Make even more informed decisions about your project with the second element of our package, the Material Cost Report. The material and installation cost is shown for each of more than 1,000 line items provided in the standard-grade Materials List, which is included with this tool. Additional space is included for estimates from contractors and subcontractors, such as for mechanical materials, which are not included in our packages.

Quote One® Summary Cost Report **$35**
Quote One® Detailed Material Cost Report **$140***
***Detailed material cost report includes the Materials List**

Learn the Basics of Building – Electrical, Pluming, Mechanical, Construction Detail Sheets
If you want to know more about building techniques—and deal more confidently with your subcontractors—we offer four useful detail sheets. These sheets provide non-plan-specific general information, but are excellent tools that will add to your understanding of Plumbing Details, Electrical Details, Construction Details, and Mechanical Details.

Electrical Detail Sheet **$14.95**
Plumbing Detail Sheet **$14.95**
Mechanical Detail Sheet **$14.95**
Construction Detail Sheet **$14.95**
SUPER VALUE SETS:
Buy any 2: $26.95; Buy any 3: $34.95; Buy All 4: $39.95

Best Value

MAKE YOUR HOME TECH-READY – HOME AUTOMATION UPGRADE

Building a new home provides a unique opportunity to wire it with a plan for future needs. A Home Automation-Ready (HA-Ready) home contains the wiring substructure of tomorrow's connected home. It means that every room—from the front porch to the backyard, and from the attic to the basement—is wired for security, lighting, telecommunications, climate control, home computer networking, whole-house audio, home theater, shade control, video surveillance, entry access control, and yes, video gaming electronic solutions.

Along with the conveniences HA-Ready homes provide, they also have a higher resale value. The Consumer Electronics Association (CEA), in conjunction with the Custom Electronic Design and Installation Association (CEDIA), have developed a TechHome™ Rating system that quantifies the value of HA-Ready homes. The rating system is gaining widespread recognition in the real estate industry.

Developed by CEDIA-certified installers, our Home Automation Upgrade package includes everything you need to work with an installer during the construction of your home. It provides a short explanation of the various subsystems, a wiring floor plan for each level of your home, a detailed materials list with estimated costs, and a list of CEDIA-certified installers in your local area.
Home Automation Upgrade **$250**

GET YOUR HOME PLANS PAID FOR!

IndyMac Bank, in partnership with Hanley Wood, will reimburse you up to $1,000 toward the cost of your home plans simply by financing the construction of your new home with IndyMac Bank Home Construction Lending.

IndyMac's construction and permanent loan is a one-time close loan, meaning that one application—and one set of closing fees—provides all the financing you need.

Apply today at www.indymacbank.com, call toll free at 1-800-847-6138, or ask a Hanley Wood customer service representative for details.

DESIGN YOUR HOME – INTERIOR AND EXTERIOR FINISHING TOUCHES

Be Your Own Interior Designer! – Home Furniture Planner

Effectively plan the space in your home using our Hands-On Home Furniture Planner. It's fun and easy—no more moving heavy pieces of furniture to see how the room will go together. The kit includes reusable peel-and-stick furniture templates that fit on a 12"x18" laminated layout board—enough space to lay out every room in your house.
Home Furniture Planning Kit **$15.95**

Enjoy the Outdoors! – Deck Plans

Many of our homes have a corresponding deck plan, sold separately, which includes a Deck Plan Frontal Sheet, Deck Framing and Floor Plans, Deck Elevations, and a Deck Materials List. A Standard Deck Details Package, also available, provides all the how-to information necessary for building any deck. Get both the Deck Plan and the Standard Deck Details Package for one low price in our Complete Deck Building Package. See the price tier chart below and call for deck plan availability.
Deck Details (only) **$14.95**
Deck Building Package . . . . **Plan price + $14.95**

Create a Professionally Designed Landscape – Landscape Plans

Many of our homes have a front-yard Landscape Plan that is complementary in design to the house plan. These comprehensive Landscape Blueprint Packages include a Frontal Sheet, Plan View, Regionalized Plant & Materials List, a sheet on Planting and Maintaining Your Landscape, Zone Maps, and a Plant Size and Description Guide. Each set of blueprints is a full 18" x 24" with clear, complete instructions in easy-to-read type. Our Landscape Plans are available with a Plant & Materials List adapted by horticultural experts to eight regions of the country. Please specify your region when ordering your plan—see region map below. Call for more information about landscape plan availability and applicable regions.

LANDSCAPE & DECK PRICE SCHEDULE

PRICE TIERS	1-SET STUDY PACKAGE	5-SET BUILDING PACKAGE	8-SET BUILDING PACKAGE	1-SET REPRODUCIBLE*
P1	$25	$55	$95	$145
P2	$45	$75	$115	$165
P3	$75	$105	$145	$195
P4	$105	$135	$175	$225
P5	$175	$205	$305	$405
P6	$215	$245	$345	$445

PRICES SUBJECT TO CHANGE   * REQUIRES A FAX NUMBER

TERMS & CONDITIONS

OUR 90-DAY EXCHANGE POLICY

BUY WITH CONFIDENCE!

Hanley Wood is committed to ensuring your satisfaction with your blueprint order, which is why we offer a 90-day exchange policy. With the exception of Reproducible Plan Package orders, we will exchange your entire first order for an equal or greater number of blueprints from our plan collection within 90 days of the original order. The entire content of your original order must be returned before an exchange will be processed. Please call our customer service department at 1-888-690-1116 for your return authorization number and shipping instructions. If the returned blueprints look used, redlined, or copied, we will not honor your exchange. Fees for exchanging your blueprints are as follows: 20% of the amount of the original order, plus the difference in cost if exchanging for a design in a higher price bracket or less the difference in cost if exchanging for a design in a lower price bracket. (Because they can be copied, Reproducible blueprints are not exchangeable or refundable.) Please call for current postage and handling prices. Shipping and handling charges are not refundable.

ARCHITECTURAL AND ENGINEERING SEALS

Some cities and states now require that a licensed architect or engineer review and "seal" a blueprint, or officially approve it, prior to construction. Prior to application for a building permit or the start of actual construction, we strongly advise that you consult your local building official who can tell you if such a review is required.

LOCAL BUILDING CODES AND ZONING REQUIREMENTS

Each plan was designed to meet or exceed the requirements of a nationally recognized model building code in effect at the time and place the plan was drawn. Typically plans designed after the year 2000 conform to the International Residential Building Code (IRC 2000 or 2003). The IRC is comprised of portions of the three major codes below. Plans drawn before 2000 conform to one of the three recognized building codes in effect at the time: Building Officials and Code Administrators (BOCA) International, Inc.;

**CALL TOLL-FREE
1-800-521-6797
OR VISIT
EPLANS.COM**

the Southern Building Code Congress International, (SBCCI) Inc.; the International Conference of Building Officials (ICBO); or the Council of American Building Officials (CABO).

Because of the great differences in geography and climate throughout the United States and Canada, each state, county, and municipality has its own building codes, zone requirements, ordinances, and building regulations. Your plan may need to be modified to comply with local requirements. In addition, you may need to obtain permits or inspections from local governments before and in the course of construction. We authorize the use of the blueprints on the express condition that you consult a local licensed architect or engineer of your choice prior to beginning construction and strictly comply with all local building codes, zoning requirements, and other applicable laws, regulations, ordinances, and requirements. Notice: Plans for homes to be built in Nevada must be redrawn by a Nevada-registered professional. Consult your local building official for more information on this subject.

TERMS AND CONDITIONS

These designs are protected under the terms of United States Copyright Law and may not be copied or reproduced in any way, by

any means, unless you have purchased a Reproducible Plan Package and signed the accompanying license to modify and copy the plan, which clearly indicates your right to modify, copy, or reproduce. We authorize the use of your chosen design as an aid in the construction of ONE (1) single- or multifamily home only. You may not use this design to build a second dwelling or multiple dwellings without purchasing another blueprint or blueprints or paying additional design fees. Multi-use fees vary by designer—please call one of experienced sales representatives for a quote.

DISCLAIMER

The designers we work with have put substantial care and effort into the creation of their blueprints. However, because we cannot provide on-site consultation, supervision, and control over actual construction, and because of the great variance in local building requirements, building practices, and soil, seismic, weather, and other conditions, WE MAKE NO WARRANTY OF ANY KIND, EXPRESS OR IMPLIED, WITH RESPECT TO THE CONTENT OR USE OF THE BLUEPRINTS, INCLUDING BUT NOT LIMITED TO ANY WARRANTY OF MERCHANTABILITY OR OF FITNESS FOR A PARTICULAR PURPOSE. ITEMS, PRICES, TERMS, AND CONDITIONS ARE SUBJECT TO CHANGE WITHOUT NOTICE.

BEFORE YOU ORDER

IMPORTANT COPYRIGHT NOTICE

From the Council of Publishing Home Designers

Blueprints for residential construction (or working drawings, as they are often called in the industry) are copyrighted intellectual property, protected under the terms of the United States Copyright Law and, therefore, cannot be copied legally for use in building. The following are some guidelines to help you get what you need to build your home, without violating copyright law:

1. HOME PLANS ARE COPYRIGHTED

Just like books, movies, and songs, home plans receive protection under the federal copyright laws. The copyright laws prevent anyone, other than the copyright owner, from reproducing, modifying, or reusing the plans or design without permission of the copyright owner.

2. DO NOT COPY DESIGNS OR FLOOR PLANS FROM ANY PUBLICATION, ELECTRONIC MEDIA, OR EXISTING HOME

It is illegal to copy, change, or redraw home designs found in a plan book, CDROM or on the Internet. The right to modify plans is one of the exclusive rights of copyright. It is also illegal to copy or redraw a constructed home that is protected by copyright, even if you have never seen the plans for the home. If you find a plan or home that you like, you must purchase a set of plans from an authorized source. The plans may not be lent, given away, or sold by the purchaser.

3. DO NOT USE PLANS TO BUILD MORE THAN ONE HOUSE

The original purchaser of house plans is typically licensed to build a single home from the plans. Building more than one home from the plans without permission is an infringement of the home designer's copyright. The purchase of a multiple-set package of plans is for the construction of a single home only. The purchase of additional sets of plans does not grant the right to construct more than one home.

4. HOUSE PLANS IN THE FORM OF BLUEPRINTS OR BLACKLINES CANNOT BE COPIED OR REPRODUCED

Plans, blueprints, or blacklines, unless they are reproducibles, cannot be copied or reproduced without prior written consent of the copyright owner. Copy shops and blueprinters are prohibited from making copies of these plans without the copyright release letter you receive with reproducible plans.

5. HOUSE PLANS IN THE FORM OF BLUEPRINTS OR BLACKLINES CANNOT BE REDRAWN

Plans cannot be modified or redrawn without first obtaining the copyright owner's permission. With your purchase of plans, you are licensed to make non-structural changes by "red-lining" the purchased plans. If you need to make structural changes or need to redraw the plans for any reason, you must purchase a reproducible set of plans (see topic 6) which includes a license to modify the plans. Blueprints do not come with a license to make structural changes or to redraw the plans. You may not reuse or sell the modified design.

6. REPRODUCIBILE HOME PLANS

Reproducible plans (for example sepias, mylars, CAD files, electronic files, and vellums) come with a license to make modifications to the plans. Once modified, the plans can be taken to a local copy shop or blueprinter to make up to 10 or 12 copies of the plans to use in the construction of a single home. Only one home can be constructed from any single purchased set of reproducible plans either in original form or as modified. The license to modify and copy must be completed and returned before the plan will be shipped.

7. MODIFIED DESIGNS CANNOT BE REUSED

Even if you are licensed to make modifications to a copyrighted design, the modified design is not free from the original designer's copyright. The sale or reuse of the modified design is prohibited. Also, be aware that any modification to plans relieves the original designer from liability for design defects and voids all warranties expressed or implied.

8. WHO IS RESPONSIBLE FOR COPYRIGHT INFRINGEMENT?

Any party who participates in a copyright violation may be responsible including the purchaser, designers, architects, engineers, drafters, homeowners, builders, contractors, sub-contractors, copy shops, blueprinters, developers, and real estate agencies. It does not matter whether or not the individual knows that a violation is being committed. Ignorance of the law is not a valid defense.

9. PLEASE RESPECT HOME DESIGN COPYRIGHTS

In the event of any suspected violation of a copyright, or if there is any uncertainty about the plans purchased, the publisher, architect, designer, or the Council of Publishing Home Designers (www.cphd.org) should be contacted before proceeding. Awards are sometimes offered for information about home design copyright infringement.

10. PENALTIES FOR INFRINGEMENT

Penalties for violating a copyright may be severe. The responsible parties are required to pay actual damages caused by the infringement (which may be substantial), plus any profits made by the infringer commissions to include all profits from the sale of any home built from an infringing design. The copyright law also allows for the recovery of statutory damages, which may be as high as $150,000 for each infringement. Finally, the infringer may be required to pay legal fees which often exceed the damages.

BLUEPRINT PRICE SCHEDULE

PRICE TIERS	1-SET STUDY PACKAGE	5-SET BUILDING PACKAGE	8-SET BUILDING PACKAGE	1-SET REPRODUCIBLE*
A1	$465	$515	$570	$695
A2	$505	$560	$615	$755
A3	$570	$625	$685	$860
A4	$615	$680	$745	$925
C1	$660	$735	$800	$990
C2	$710	$785	$845	$1,055
C3	$775	$835	$900	$1,135
C4	$830	$905	$960	$1,215
L1	$920	$1,020	$1,105	$1,375
L2	$1,000	$1,095	$1,185	$1,500
L3	$1,105	$1,210	$1,310	$1,650
L4	$1,220	$1,335	$1,425	$1,830
SQ1				.40/SQ. FT.
SQ3				.55/SQ. FT.
SQ5				.80/SQ. FT.
SQ7				$1.00 / SQ. FT.
SQ9				$1.25 / SQ. FT.
SQ11				$1.50 / SQ. FT.

PRICES SUBJECT TO CHANGE

* REQUIRES A FAX NUMBER

PLAN #	PRICE TIER	PAGE	MATERIALS LIST	QUOTE ONE®	DECK	DECK PRICE	LANDSCAPE	LANDSCAPE PRICE	REGIONS
HPK2400001	C4	12							
HPK2400002	C3	17	Y						
HPK2400003	C4	18							
HPK2400004	C4	19							
HPK2400005	SQ1	20							
HPK2400006	SQ1	21	Y						
HPK2400007	SQ1	22	Y	Y			OLA001	P3	123568
HPK2400008	C4	23							
HPK2400009	SQ3	24							
HPK2400010	C3	25							
HPK2400011	L1	26							
HPK2400012	SQ7	27							
HPK2400013	L1	28	Y						
HPK2400014	C4	29							
HPK2400015	SQ7	30	Y						
HPK2400016	C4	31							
HPK2400017	L1	32							
HPK2400018	L1	33	Y						
HPK2400019	SQ1	34	Y						
HPK2400020	C4	35	Y						
HPK2400021	SQ3	36							
HPK2400022	SQ1	37	Y						
HPK2400023	SQ7	38	Y						
HPK2400024	L1	39	Y						
HPK2400025	SQ7	40							
HPK2400026	SQ7	41							
HPK2400027	SQ5	42							
HPK2400028	SQ1	43							
HPK2400029	SQ1	44	Y						
HPK2400030	C4	45	Y						
HPK2400031	SQ7	46	Y						
HPK2400032	SQ7	47							
HPK2400033	L3	48	Y						
HPK2400034	SQ7	49	Y						
HPK2400035	L1	50	Y						
HPK2400036	L3	51	Y						
HPK2400037	SQ7	52							
HPK2400038	SQ7	53							
HPK2400039	L1	54	Y						
HPK2400040	SQ7	55							
HPK2400041	SQ1	56							
HPK2400042	L3	57							
HPK2400043	SQ3	58	Y						
HPK2400044	L3	59							
HPK2400045	SQ7	60	Y						
HPK2400046	SQ7	61							
HPK2400047	SQ1	62	Y	Y			OLA028	P4	12345678
HPK2400048	SQ7	63							
HPK2400049	SQ7	64	Y						
HPK2400050	L4	65							

PLAN #	PRICE TIER	PAGE	MATERIALS LIST	QUOTE ONE®	DECK	DECK PRICE	LANDSCAPE	LANDSCAPE PRICE	REGIONS
HPK2400051	SQ1	66	Y						
HPK2400052	SQ1	67	Y						
HPK2400053	SQ3	68							
HPK2400054	L4	69							
HPK2400055	L4	70	Y						
HPK2400056	L4	71							
HPK2400057	SQ1	72	Y						
HPK2400058	C2	77	Y						
HPK2400059	C4	78							
HPK2400060	C2	79							
HPK2400061	SQ3	80							
HPK2400062	C3	81	Y						
HPK2400063	C2	82							
HPK2400064	C2	83							
HPK2400065	C3	84	Y						
HPK2400066	SQ3	85							
HPK2400067	C3	86	Y						
HPK2400068	C3	87							
HPK2400069	C4	88							
HPK2400070	C3	89	Y						
HPK2400071	C2	90							
HPK2400072	C3	91	Y						
HPK2400073	C2	92							
HPK2400074	C4	93							
HPK2400075	C3	94							
HPK2400076	C4	95							
HPK2400077	C3	96	Y						
HPK2400078	C3	97	Y						
HPK2400079	C3	98							
HPK2400080	C2	99					OLA008	P4	1234568
HPK2400081	C4	100							
HPK2400082	C3	101	Y						
HPK2400083	L2	102							
HPK2400084	C4	103	Y						
HPK2400085	C3	104					OLA017	P3	123568
HPK2400086	C3	105							
HPK2400087	C4	106	Y						
HPK2400088	L1	107							
HPK2400089	SQ1	108							
HPK2400090	C3	109	Y						
HPK2400091	SQ1	110							
HPK2400092	SQ1	111							
HPK2400093	SQ1	112							
HPK2400094	C4	113							
HPK2400095	L1	114							
HPK2400096	L2	115							
HPK2400097	C4	116	Y						
HPK2400098	C4	117							
HPK2400099	L1	118							
HPK2400100	L1	119							
HPK2400101	SQ3	120							
HPK2400102	SQ3	121							
HPK2400103	SQ3	122							
HPK2400104	SQ1	123							
HPK2400105	L1	124	Y	Y					
HPK2400106	SQ1	125	Y						
HPK2400107	SQ1	126	Y						
HPK2400108	L1	131							
HPK2400109	C4	132							
HPK2400110	C4	133	Y	Y					
HPK2400111	C2	134	Y						
HPK2400112	C2	135							
HPK2400113	L1	136	Y						
HPK2400114	C3	137							
HPK2400115	SQ3	138							
HPK2400116	C3	139	Y						
HPK2400117	C4	140							
HPK2400118	C2	141							
HPK2400119	SQ1	142	Y						
HPK2400120	C3	143	Y	Y			OLA016	P4	1234568
HPK2400121	C3	144	Y	Y			OLA017	P3	123568
HPK2400122	L1	145							
HPK2400123	SQ1	146							
HPK2400124	L1	147							
HPK2400125	C4	148							
HPK2400126	L1	149	Y						
HPK2400127	C3	150	Y						
HPK2400128	L1	151							
HPK2400129	L1	152	Y	Y	ODA002	D1	OLA015	P4	123568
HPK2400130	C4	153	Y	Y	ODA012	D2	OLA016	P4	1234568
HPK2400131	C4	154	Y						
HPK2400132	L2	155	Y	Y	ODA012	D2	OLA036	P4	12356
HPK2400133	C4	156	Y	Y	ODA008	D2	OLA017	P3	123568
HPK2400134	L1	157							
HPK2400135	SQ1	158	Y						
HPK2400136	L2	159							
HPK2400137	L1	160							
HPK2400138	SQ3	161							
HPK2400139	L1	162							
HPK2400140	L1	163	Y	Y	ODA006	D1	OLA019	P4	1234568
HPK2400141	SQ1	164							
HPK2400142	L2	165	Y						
HPK2400143	C4	166							
HPK2400144	L2	167							
HPK2400145	L1	168							
HPK2400146	SQ1	169							
HPK2400147	L1	170							
HPK2400148	L1	171	Y						
HPK2400149	SQ1	172	Y						
HPK2400150	SQ1	173							
HPK2400151	L3	174							
HPK2400152	SQ1	175							
HPK2400153	L1	176	Y						
HPK2400154	L1	177							
HPK2400155	L4	178							
HPK2400156	SQ1	179	Y				OLA017	P3	123568
HPK2400157	L3	180							
HPK2400158	SQ1	181	Y						

Idyllic Escapes

Take the plunge and start building your perfect vacation home. No matter if you are seeking a breathtaking view, a relaxing retreat or a cozy cabin, Hanley Wood has the house plan to fit your every fantasy.

Homes with a View

175 Plans for Golf-Course, Waterfront and Mountain Homes: This stunning collection features homes as magnificent as the vistas they showcase. A 32-page, full-color gallery showcases the most spectacular homes—all designed specifically to accent the natural beauty of their surrounding landscapes.

$14.95 U.S. (*192 pages*)
ISBN 1-931131-25-2

Vacation & Second Homes, 3rd Ed.

430 House Plans for Retreats and Getaways: Visit the cutting edge of home design in this fresh portfolio of getaway plans—ready to build anywhere. From sprawling haciendas to small rustic cabins, this collection takes on your wildest dreams with designs suited for waterfronts, cliffsides, or wide-open spaces.

$11.95 U.S. (*288 pages*)
ISBN 1-931131-37-6

Cool Cottages

245 Delightful Retreats
825 to 3,500 square feet: Cozy, inviting house plans designed to provide the ideal escape from the stress of daily life. This charming compilation offers perfect hideaways for every locale: mountaintops to foothills, woodlands to everglades.

$10.95 U.S. (*256 pages*)
ISBN 1-881955-91-5

Fine Living

130 Home Designs with Luxury Amenities: The homes in this collection offer lovely exteriors, flowing floor plans and ample interior space, plus a stunning array of amenities that goes above and beyond standard designs. This title features gorgeous full-color photos, tips on furnishing and decorating as well as an extensive reference section packed with inspiring ideas.

$17.95 U.S. (*192 pages*)
ISBN 1-931131-24-4

Waterfront Homes, 2nd Ed.

189 Home Plans for River, Lake or Sea: A beautiful waterfront setting calls for a beautiful home. Whether you are looking for a year-round home or a vacation getaway, this is a fantastic collection of home plans to choose from.

$10.95 U.S. (*208 pages*)
ISBN 1-931131-28-7

Getaway Plans

250 Home Plans for Cottages, Bungalows & Capes: This is the perfect volume for anyone looking to create their own relaxing place to escape life's pressures—whether it's a vacation home or primary residence! Also included, tips to create a comfortable, yet beautiful atmosphere in a small space.

$9.95 U.S. (*448 pages*)
ISBN 1-881955-97-4

Hanley Wood Books

One Thomas Circle, NW | Suite 600 | Washington, DC 20005
877.447.5450 | www.hanleywoodbooks.com

HPK2